101 WAYS

to Make **Studying** Easier and Faster for

High School
Students

What Every Student Needs to Know Explained Simply

By Janet Engel

101 WAYS TO MAKE STUDYING EASIER AND FASTER FOR HIGH SCHOOL STUDENTS: WHAT EVERY STUDENT NEEDS TO KNOW EXPLAINED SIMPLY

ISBN-13: 978-1-60138-217-7   ISBN-10: 1-60138-217-0

Library of Congress Cataloging-in-Publication Data

Engle, Janet.
  101 ways to make studying easier and faster for high school students : what every student needs to know explained simply / by Janet Engle.
      p. cm.
  Includes bibliographical references and index.
  ISBN-13: 978-1-60138-217-7 (alk. paper)
  ISBN-10: 1-60138-217-0 (alk. paper)
  1. Study skills--Handbooks, manuals, etc. 2. High school students--Handbooks, manuals, etc. I. Title. II. Title: One hundred one ways to make studying easier and faster for high school students. III. Title: One hundred and one ways to make studying easier and faster for high school students.

  LB1601.E54 2008
  373.13'0281--dc22
                          2008023670

Printed on Recycled Paper

INTERIOR LAYOUT DESIGN: Vickie Taylor • vtaylor@atlantic-pub.com

Printed in the United States

We recently lost our beloved pet "Bear," who was not only our best and dearest friend but also the "Vice President of Sunshine" here at Atlantic Publishing. He did not receive a salary but worked tirelessly 24 hours a day to please his parents. Bear was a rescue dog that turned around and showered myself, my wife Sherri, his grandparents Jean, Bob, and Nancy and every person and animal he met (maybe not rabbits) with friendship and love. He made a lot of people smile every day.

We wanted you to know that a portion of the profits of this book will be donated to The Humane Society of the United States.

–Douglas & Sherri Brown

THE HUMANE SOCIETY
OF THE UNITED STATES ©

The human-animal bond is as old as human history. We cherish our animal companions for their unconditional affection and acceptance. We feel a thrill when we glimpse wild creatures in their natural habitat or in our own backyard.

Unfortunately, the human-animal bond has at times been weakened. Humans have exploited some animal species to the point of extinction.

The Humane Society of the United States makes a difference in the lives of animals here at home and worldwide. The HSUS is dedicated to creating a world where our relationship with animals is guided by compassion. We seek a truly humane society in which animals are respected for their intrinsic value, and where the human-animal bond is strong.

Want to help animals? We have plenty of suggestions. Adopt a pet from a local shelter, join The Humane Society and be a part of our work to help companion animals and wildlife. You will be funding our educational, legislative, investigative, and outreach projects in the U.S. and across the globe.

Or perhaps you'd like to make a memorial donation in honor of a pet, friend, or relative? You can through our Kindred Spirits program. And if you'd like to contribute in a more structured way, our Planned Giving Office has suggestions about estate planning, annuities, and even gifts of stock that avoid capital gains taxes.

Maybe you have land that you would like to preserve as a lasting habitat for wildlife. Our Wildlife Land Trust can help you. Perhaps the land you want to share is a backyard — that's enough. Our Urban Wildlife Sanctuary Program will show you how to create a habitat for your wild neighbors.

So you see, it's easy to help animals. And The HSUS is here to help.

The Humane Society of the United States
2100 L Street NW
Washington, DC 20037
202-452-1100
www.hsus.org

TABLE OF CONTENTS

INTRODUCTION

The teenage years are often referred to as the best time of your life — frequently by adults who graduated too long ago to remember what high school is truly like.

In addition to being a chance to experiment with identities, branch out socially, and learn new skills and ideas, high school can be stressful and exhausting. Students may be expected to juggle school, work, extra-curricular activities, after-school jobs, and household chores, but they are seldom given the tools they need for success.

When I was in high school, I managed to get good grades despite horrible study habits. Some late nights at the dinner table and early mornings at the school library, combined with a natural talent for quick memorization, were sufficient for most tests and assignments. When semester exams rolled around, though, I would realize just how little I had truly learned during those haphazard study sessions. I always felt as if I was looking at the material for the first time, and my exam grades would reflect that I had never mastered the concepts.

Projects and term papers were equally unsuited to my "cram the night before" study technique. Luckily for my report card, my teachers stopped assigning long-term homework around my sophomore year. Maybe they were as tired of grading half-completed, poorly-organized work as my classmates and I were of doing it.

My poor time-management and study habits did not become real problems until I started college. Between lectures, laboratories, and readings, I had to learn more information than I could possibly memorize in one night. Most of my classmates seemed much more skilled at keeping on top of their work, and the professors did not share my high school teachers' avoidance of long-term assignments.

I had to learn how to study, so I took every time-management and study-skills workshop I could find. Because I had to manage a full class load and a part-time job, I quickly figured out which techniques gave the best results in the least amount of time.

The ability to study does not come naturally to all students. If you have been making good grades by cramming the nights before your tests, you may wonder why you should take the time to change your habits. If you spend hours each night with your textbooks but do not make the grades you want, you may wonder if there is any hope.

The techniques in this book can help you. The tips will help you categorize your tasks in order of importance, organize your work area, and complete more schoolwork in less time:

By learning how to study more efficiently and effectively, you will be able to manage your responsibilities with less stress.

High school can be the best years of your life. The study and time management skills you develop now will help you prepare for success in college and throughout your career.

Study Easier & Faster

Unless you recognize the long-term consequences of your academic performance in high school, you may find it difficult to put in the time and effort needed to succeed.

The grades you make now can shape your life in many ways. States and schools may set eligibility requirements for participating in sports and other extracurricular activities. If your grade point average drops too low, you may not be able to pay basketball, try out for the spring musical, or represent your school at the next art show.

Some localities do not allow students to hold summer or after-school jobs if their grades fall below a certain level. Even if you meet the minimum requirements, employers may be hesitant to hire students who have trouble managing their class work. If you rely on employment to pay for a car, spending money, or to help your family, low grades can limit your earning potential.

Colleges look at high-school transcripts to determine which students they will accept. Once you are accepted at a school, low grades in high school may prevent you from enrolling in advanced classes, declaring a major, participating in a sport, or receiving financial aid.

Barriers to Effective Studying

The grades you receive in high school can influence your life long after you receive a report card. Even after you graduate, grades can still have an impact on your life. With so much on the line, why do some students receive lower grades than they want?

Not Enough Hours in the Day

Between work, after-school activities, family responsibilities, and socializing, students may believe they do not have the time to complete assignments and master information. Students may fit a few minutes of studying in between other commitments, cram for tests at the last minute, or decide to skip an assignment altogether rather than do a bad job on it.

Poor Concentration

After they have carved out a block of study time and sit down with their notes and textbooks, some students find it difficult to stay on task. They may spend their study session staring out the window, adjusting the thermostat, or doodling in their notebook.

Low Motivation

For some students, the hardest part of studying is getting started. Even if they recognize the importance of good grades, they find it hard to turn off the television and crack open the books. They may rationalize that they are too busy to fit it into their schedules.

The Need to Be Perfect

Some students sabotage their own study efforts by trying to make everything just right. These students may spend more time organizing their math notebook than doing math problems. They may expend so much energy choosing the perfect cover, font, and layout for their English term paper that they are too exhausted to truly research and write the paper.

Studying the Wrong Things

If your grades do not reflect the hours you spend in focused study, you may be studying the wrong information. Instead of making more time to work, you may need to take the time to learn better study techniques.

Break through the Barriers

If one or more of the above obstacles is keeping you from academic success, you have the power to break down those barriers, learn to study efficiently and effectively, and per your grades.

If you have trouble fitting study time into your schedule, the tips in this book can help you improve your time-management skills and help you learn to get more work finished in less time. If you find it difficult to ignore the view outside your window, the paperback in your backpack, or the reruns on television, this book can help you discover ways to focus and make the most of each study session. If low motivation is causing low grades, this book can show you how to set intermediate goals, reward yourself for progress, and plan study sessions that are fast, fun, and easy. If you find yourself unable to study because your desk accessories are not color-coordinated, you will find tips that help you learn to control your perfectionism. If you always seem to study the wrong things, the techniques described can help you recognize what sections of your textbook you should focus on, and what you can safely ignore.

Basic Studying Tips

You may not be able to change your study habits overnight, but by using the tips in this book, you should see progress over the course of the next semester.

Tip 1: Devote 15 minutes every day to improving your study skills or preparing to study.

Fifteen minutes is enough time to make progress, but not so long that it becomes another cause of stress in your busy life. A quarter of an hour may not sound like much time, but it should be enough to do at least one of these tasks:

- Read a few pages of this book.

- Review your calendar.

- Clear old papers from your desk.

- Restock your pencil jar.

- File the day's papers.

- Make a "to-do" list for the evening's study session.

- Organize your bookcase.

- Vacuum and dust your work area.

☙ Take a short walk to clear your mind.

☙ Change into comfortable clothing.

☙ Reflect on study changes you have already made.

Forming good study habits is a big project, but this technique breaks it into manageable chunks. You can also apply this tip to other large projects, such as:

☙ Researching a term paper

☙ Reading a novel

☙ Memorizing a foreign language vocabulary list

☙ Learning a difficult piece of music

☙ Creating a work area

☙ Preparing for final exams

The trick here is to commit to 15 minutes, and no more than 15 minutes, every single day.

Tip 2: Concentrate on the goal, not the process.

Decide what you want to gain from your study time. Your goals may include:

☙ Earning better grades

☙ Mastering information instead of just learning it for tests

- Studying more efficiently

- Preparing for standardized tests

- Practicing skills introduced in class

- Completing assignments on time and to the best of your ability

The tips in this book, combined with focus and steady work, can help you reach your academic goals. The key to success is to remember your long-term objectives. Make sure the work you do every day targets your goals. Do not allow yourself to get sidetracked by the process of studying. The purpose of each session should be to study as effectively as possible, not to impress people with your overly packed calendar, sound like a martyr when you complain about how long you studied for a test, create the most high-tech workspace, or have an excuse not to do chores.

Tip 3: Have a daily plan.

Keep a running list of what you have to do every day. Having a daily plan will help you remember small tasks, and it can help you stay motivated and focused. Even if you only have five or 10 minutes between classes or before basketball practice, odds are there is something on your list you can do. Cross off each task as it is completed, and by the end of the day, you will see just how much you have accomplished.

You can keep your to-do list on a scrap sheet of paper, but a small spiral notebook that can slip into your backpack or binder is less likely to be lost and will let you review your progress. Use a paperclip to mark your place so that you can turn to the current page quickly whenever you need to make an entry.

Tip 4: Minimize surprises.

Cramming is one of the least effective ways to study. Reduce the need to pull all-nighters by writing deadlines and test dates on a yearly wall calendar. Hang the calendar in a conspicuous place.

Refer to your calendar before you go to school every morning and again when you get home. Do not fill this calendar with motivational quotes, daily assignments, or doodles. Those can go on your daily to-do list. Keep this calendar efficient and effective. At a glance, you should be able to see if any presentations, exams, papers, or projects are approaching.

Write exam dates and deadlines for long-term projects on your wall calendar as soon as possible. Homework due the next morning should not go on this calendar, but anything more than a day away should be included. If you are involved in any sports, clubs, or activities, use your calendar to keep track of competitions, tryouts, rehearsals, and meetings. In addition, use it to manage your social and personal obligations such as parties, doctors' appointments, school holidays, and family gatherings.

Keeping a yearly calendar has several benefits, including:

More time: You will not waste time wondering why January 18 sounds familiar or flipping through your notebook to find out when your biology lab report is due.

Less double booking: You will know not to schedule a baby-sitting job on the same evening you have a soccer match.

Fewer papers to juggle: Whenever you are given a schedule for a class or activity, immediately transfer the information to your calendar and dispose of the extra paper.

Better coordination between multiple projects: If you know that All-State band auditions are the evening before your English term paper is due, you will know that you will have limited time to work on the paper at the last minute. The earlier you recognize a possible conflict, the more time you have to work out a solution.

More opportunities: If you notice a two-week block without any exams or events, you may decide to schedule a new activity or take advantage of the lull to get ahead on class readings or a major assignment.

Less stress: Because you know what is coming up, you will not have to worry about forgetting an exam or deadline. Being more relaxed will help you study more efficiently.

Tip 5: Take breaks.

Studying is hard work. You need more time to process and learn information if you are mentally fatigued. When you are well-rested, you are better able to understand difficult concepts, solve problems, and retain facts. Scheduling five minutes of break time for every 15 minutes you study can help you stay mentally sharp and ready to keep studying.

Try to change gears during your breaks. Let your brain relax a few minutes, but do not start anything that will take longer than the time you have allotted. During your break time, you may find it refreshing to:

- Fix yourself a cup of tea.

- Perform a set of yoga poses.

- Arrange the supplies you will need to study the next subject.

- Check your e-mail.

- Brush your teeth.

- Meditate.

- Walk outside and breathe some fresh air.

- Flip through a magazine.

- Sharpen your pencil.

- Eat a quick snack.

- Pet a dog or cat.

These suggestions may not be good break-time choices for everyone. If you have to check your favorite blog and respond to a few posts on a message board each time you touch the computer, a quick e-mail check may turn into a half-hour spent playing on the Internet. Avoid any activities that you find hard to tear yourself away from. Activities that are likely to take longer than five minutes include:

- Watching television

- Preparing or eating a meal

- Talking on the telephone

- Returning text messages

- Reading a book

- Taking a walk

- Napping

- Cleaning

- Doing laundry

- Tweaking a Web site

- Practicing a musical instrument

- Taking a bath

You may find it useful to study a different subject after each break, even if it means you have to revisit a topic later in your study session. Varying subjects can help you avoid becoming bored, and may help you approach challenging problems with fresh eyes and remember more information.

A study session for a student who schedules a short break every 15 minutes might look like this:

7:20 to 7:35 – Math homework

7:35 to 7:40 – Sit ups and light stretches

7:40 to 7:55 – Spanish homework

7:55 to 8:00 – Pop a bag of popcorn, pour a glass of soda

8:00 to 8:15 – Finish math homework, review history notes

8:15 to 8:20 – Take out trash

8:20 to 8:35 – Finish Spanish homework, outline history chapter

In a little over an hour, the student in the example prepared work for three classes, exercised, prepared a snack, and completed a chore. By rotating subjects and taking well-timed breaks, the student accomplished more with less mental fatigue.

Tip 6: Use a timer.

Pulling yourself away from a break can be difficult. Even if you have the full intention to return to your desk immediately after you have a snack at the kitchen table, chat with a friend, or play a quick video, five minutes can go by quickly. Before you know it, you can spend your entire study session participating in non-academic activities.

A simple kitchen timer can help keep you honest about your break times. Set your timer for five minutes and commit to returning to your work when the alarm rings.

A timer is also helpful to count down the minutes between breaks. If your timer becomes a distraction and you find yourself watching the clock instead of studying, invest in a loud unit that you can keep in a separate room or a portable timer that fits in your pocket. Timers that can be set to vibrate instead of ringing are useful if you study in a public area like a library or share a room with someone who is bothered by the alarm.

Tip 7: Do not procrastinate.

Start studying for a test as soon as possible. The earlier you begin, the less work you will have to do each day to understand the material to the best of your abilities.

The first step when preparing for an exam is to define study tasks. Each task should have a definite end. Write the tasks down and tape the list to your desk. Devote one or two 15-minute chunks of your nightly session to working on the project. Cross off each task as you complete it.

A student who needs to study for a history final exam might divide the project into the following list of tasks:

History Final Exam Tasks
1. Gather and sort previous exams, assignments and notes.
2. Review notes for Chapter 1
3. Review notes for Chapter 2
4. Review notes for Chapter 3
5. Review assignments for Chapters 1-3
6. Review Exam 1
7. Review notes for Chapter 4
8. Review notes for Chapter 5
9. Review notes for Chapter 6
10. Review assignments for Chapters 4-6
11. Review Exam 2
12. Review notes for Chapter 7
13. Review notes for Chapter 8
14. Review notes for Chapter 9

History Final Exam Tasks
15. Review assignments for Chapters 7-9
16. Review Exam 3
17. Take practice final exam
18. Look up answers to practice final exam
19. Review practice final exam, list sections that need more attention
20. Take notes on problem sections identified by practice final exam
21. List key facts to remember for exam
22. Create flash cards for key facts
23. Review flash cards
24. Create key fact quiz
25. Take and review answers to key fact quiz

A student who waits until the day before the exam to start studying will have a difficult time completing all the tasks.

Once you have listed the study tasks, count how many days you will have to work on the project. Use the list of tasks to make a daily study schedule.

A student who has five days to study for a history final exam might create the following daily study schedule.

History Final Exam Five-Day Study Schedule
Day 1
1. Gather and sort previous exams, assignments and notes.
2. Review notes for Chapter 1
3. Review notes for Chapter 2
4. Review notes for Chapter 3
5. Review assignments for Chapters 1-3

History Final Exam Five-Day Study Schedule

6. Review Exam 1

Day 2

7. Review notes for Chapter 4

8. Review notes for Chapter 5

9. Review notes for Chapter 6

10. Review assignments for Chapters 4-6

11. Review Exam 2

Day 3

12. Review notes for Chapter 7

13. Review notes for Chapter 8

14. Review notes for Chapter 9

15. Review assignments for Chapters 7-9

16. Review Exam 3

Day 4

17. Take practice final exam

18. Look up answers to practice final exam

19. Review practice final exam, list sections that need more attention

20. Take notes on problem sections identified by practice final exam

Day 5

21. List key facts to remember for exam

22. Create flash cards for key facts

23. Review flash cards

24. Create key fact quiz

25. Take and review answers to key fact quiz

If the student allows 10 days to prepare for the exam, the daily study schedule becomes more relaxed.

History Final Exam 10-Day Study Schedule

Day 1

1. Gather and sort previous exams, assignments and notes.

2. Review notes for Chapter 1

3. Review notes for Chapter 2

4. Review notes for Chapter 3

Day 2

5. Review assignments for Chapters 1-3

6. Review Exam 1

Day 3

7. Review notes for Chapter 4

8. Review notes for Chapter 5

9. Review notes for Chapter 6

Day 4

10. Review assignments for Chapters 4-6

11. Review Exam 2

Day 5

12. Review notes for Chapter 7

13. Review notes for Chapter 8

14. Review notes for Chapter 9

Day 6

15. Review assignments for Chapters 7-9

16. Review Exam 3

Day 7

17. Take practice final exam

18. Look up answers to practice final exam

Day 8

19. Review practice final exam, list sections that need more attention

History Final Exam 10-Day Study Schedule
20. Take notes on problem sections identified by practice final exam
Day 9
21. List key facts to remember for exam
22. Create flash cards for key facts
Day 10
23. Review flash cards
24. Create key fact quiz
25. Take and review answers to key fact quiz

The sample study schedules show that the student who waits to study for the exam will have to fit more tasks into each study session. The earlier preparations for the exam begin, the more likely the student is to face the test relaxed and prepared.

Tip 8: Cut yourself some slack.

Improving your time-management and study skills involves mastering new learning techniques and developing many different habits. If you expect to incorporate all the tips into your study sessions right away, then you may be setting yourself up for failure.

Give yourself time to try out different study methods. Learn what works best for you and develop your own variations. If you put off preparing for a math test until the last minute, do not use the lapse as an excuse to abandon your efforts. Even the most consistently high-achieving students occasionally overestimate their understanding of a topic and under-prepare for a test.

Occasional academic disappointments are inevitable, but they do not have to be negative. An important step in success is learning to spin setbacks into opportunities. The following chart shows positive and non-productive responses to common difficulties.

Reacting to Academic Problems		
Situation	Negative Reaction	Positive Reaction
You fail the first math test of the year.	You decide this proves you are just no good at math and resign yourself to summer school.	You ask the teacher to help you identify patterns in your wrong answers and ask for additional exercises to help you better understand the concepts that gave you trouble.
During English class, the teacher passes out copies of your latest essay as an example of poor writing.	Crumble the paper and toss it in the garbage can on your way out of the classroom.	Invest in a basic writing style guide and devote a 15-minute block of your daily study session to improving your writing skills.
You are disappointed in your score on a college entrance standardized test.	Lower your expectations about what colleges you will be accepted to.	Read about test-taking strategies and sign up for the next testing date.
The science fair is a week away and you have not decided on a topic yet.	Search the Internet for something that looks good. Change some data points and turn the work in as your own.	List what tasks need to be completed, create a study schedule, and get to work.
You stuck to a reasonable study schedule for two weeks to prepare for your Spanish test, but received a lower grade than your friend who barely studied.	Announce that studying does not work and vow to never waste that much time again.	Remind yourself of your long-term objectives and try not to think of academic performance as a competition.

Becoming angry if you make a mistake and wallowing in self-pity when you work hard but still receive a bad grade are destructive habits. They waste time, undermine your self-confidence, and discourage you from tackling new challenges.

Make Time to Study

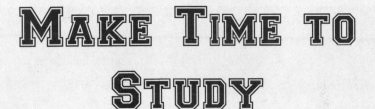

Most children do not have to worry about time. At school, teachers tell them when to read and when to put their books away. At home, a parent or guardian tells them when it is time to do their homework, practice piano, get ready for a baseball game, brush their teeth, and go to bed.

High school may be the first time that you are responsible for managing your own time. Conversely, you may have been handed the freedom to decide how to spend your hours without the tools needed to use that privilege wisely. To get the most out of the techniques in this book and improve your academic performance, you should schedule a regular study time. This is one way to responsibly handle the freedom of choosing how to spend your time wisely.

Time Management a Lifelong Skill

When you learn about the genitive case in German or the steps in mitosis, you may struggle to understand how these concepts will be important in your life after high school.

Although you can never know if your life path will take you to Munich or medical school, time management is a skill with direct real-world applications. The ability to schedule multiple tasks will benefit you no matter what career you choose.

The following table lists some professions and summarizes ways each may need to use time management skills.

Time Management in the Real World	
Physician	Coordinates patient appointments, consultations with other healthcare providers, administrative responsibilities, and research.
Civil Engineer	Reviews blueprints and notes between calls to the construction crew and architect.
Technical Writer	Revises an article for corporate newsletter while waiting for a telephone call from an interviewee.
Hospital Nurse	Plans administrative activities around patients' medication and treatment schedules.
High School Band Teacher	Decides on ensemble's concert selections while music theory class takes a quiz.
Construction Superintendent	Schedules concrete deliveries around traffic patterns and work progress so that the concrete arrives fresh just as the crew needs it.
Retail Manager	During slow sales periods, creates weekly work schedule and starts daily accounting activities. If needed, helps staff on the sales floor.

Time management includes planning tasks based on their importance, how much time they require, how time dependent they are, their interaction with other tasks, and the time window available. A proficient time manager is able to get more work completed in a shorter amount of time. For the high school student, this means being able to balance studying, family responsibilities, after-school activities, and a social life.

How Long Does it Take to Study?

A nightly study session may sound like a good idea in theory, but you may be wondering how you will ever fit it into your schedule. If you use the techniques in this book and commit to studying every night, you may be surprised at how little time it takes to complete your assignments.

The main reason that students do not study is not that they do not have enough time; it is that they would rather be doing something else. Consider a student who has a French test in two weeks. We know from the last chapter that the earlier the student starts studying for the test, the fewer tasks will need to be completed each day. The French student, on the other hand, sees the test as a low priority because it is far away. He would rather watch television or read a book than take 15 minutes to study for the test. A week and a half later, the test becomes more important. By that time, the student will need several hours to prepare. He will most likely find it more difficult to fit a three-hour block of study time into his schedule than several 15-minute blocks.

The amount of time you should devote to your regular study session depends on many factors, including:

- The difficulty of the material you are studying

- How well you can focus on the material

- Your ability to memorize

- Your ability to internalize the concepts you are learning about

- Upcoming exams and assignments

- Your reading speed

Study time is a personal thing. What one student can learn in 10 minutes might take another student half an hour. Studying is a skill, like riding a bicycle or playing a scale on the guitar. The more you practice and experiment with different techniques, the less time you will need.

TIME IS MONEY

Like money, time can be saved and invested. You can easily spend $5 a week on soft drinks after school, which does not sound like much. But, if you saved it in a box under your bed, after a year you would have $260. If you invested the money in a savings account or certificate of deposit, you would have even more.

Time is a commodity. Every day, you have a certain amount of time to divide among all the activities you want or need to do. You may choose to spend the 15 minutes before you go to field hockey practice flipping through the television channels, or you could use it to start your algebra homework.

Good time managers do not make their decisions based on which activity is easiest or the most fun, but on which is the best investment. Sometimes this is not an obvious choice. For example, you may benefit more from relaxing before a physics test than from cramming in a few minutes of extra study time.

Effective time managers consider many things when deciding how to invest their minutes. These factors include:

Current level of preparation: If you are nearly finished with your computer science presentation, you may decide that your time would be better spent by starting your geometry homework.

Desired level of preparation: If you find geology difficult, you may want to become more familiar with the material before a test or lecture.

Amount of time available to devote to the task: Some tasks are better suited to short periods of time.

Availability of supplies: You may not be able to complete some tasks without the right materials. For example, if you need to outline your psychology paper, you may need to have your research notes available.

Environment: Sometimes, your location may limit your choices. Even if your highest priority is to practice your French pronunciation, if you are at the library, you may need to choose a different task.

Distraction level: If the answers you should have included on your American literature test keep running through your head, you may not be able to focus on your chemistry homework. If a trip to the gym will clear your mind and help you concentrate, it may be a better time investment.

Despite other tasks that need to be completed, looming deadlines can trump all other considerations. Even if you are in the mood to jump ahead in your art history reading, have the needed supplies available, are in a suitable location, and have plenty of time to devote to the subject, it might be a better investment to study for the next day's journalism exam.

Effective time management involves weighing the potential benefits of different tasks. Short-term advantages of an activity might include:

- Enjoyment
- Relaxation
- Comfort
- Satisfaction

Long-term benefits include:

- Higher grades
- Better health
- Increased understanding
- Enhanced reputation
- Better preparation for future study
- Increased earning potential

A task may have both short- and long-term benefits. For example, a three-mile run around the neighborhood can be both relaxing and improve your health. A good job on a painting can be satisfying and result in a high grade in art class. Effective time managers balance short- and long-term benefits when scheduling tasks.

Tip 9: Identify tasks with primarily short-term benefits.

An activity that has no or few long-term benefits is unlikely to be a good time investment. Some common tasks that typically offer low returns include:

- Flipping through the television channels
- Eating out of boredom
- Gossiping on the telephone
- Commenting on Internet chat rooms, blogs, or discussion boards

≋   Playing video games

≋   Reorganizing items that are already tidy

Students may fill up their schedule with these activities to the point there is no room for activities with long-term benefits. An important step in effective time management is to identify these time wasters. One way to do this is to keep a detailed activity journal for several days. Make three or four copies of the sample journal below and track what you do when you are not at school, work, or an after-school activity.

Activity Journal	
2:30-2:45	
2:45-3:00	
3:00-3:15	
3:15-3:30	
3:30-3:45	
3:45-4:00	
4:00-4:15	
4:15-4:30	
4:30-4:45	
4:45-5:00	
5:00-5:15	
5:15-5:30	
5:30-5:45	
5:45-:6:00	
6:00-6:15	
6:15-6:30	
6:30-6:45	
6:45-7:00	
7:00-7:15	
7:15-7:30	
7:30-7:45	

Activity Journal
7:45-8:00	
8:00-8:15	
8:15-8:30	
8:30-8:45	
8:45-9:00	
9:00-9:15	
9:15-9:30	
9:30-9:45	
9:45-10:00	

Make a list of each task in your activity journal. Think about the short- and long-term benefits of each entry and write them in the following worksheet. Add up the total amount of time you engaged in each activity and divide by the number of days you maintained the journal. Write this average in the "Minutes Per Day" column of the "Activities and Benefits Worksheet."

Activities and Benefits Worksheet			
Activity	Minutes Per Day	Short-term Benefits	Long-term Benefits

Be honest with yourself when completing this exercise. The goal is to identify ways you can better manage your time, not to justify the things you do that waste time. Posting on an Internet discussion board does not hone your debating skills. Watching a celebrity gossip show on television does not help you stay abreast of current popular culture.

The sample "Activities and Benefits Worksheet" below shows some typical activities that may have appeared in your journal.

Activities and Benefits Worksheet			
Activity	Minutes Per Day	Short-term Benefits	Long-term Benefits
Watching TV	120	• Enjoyment • Relaxation	
Bathing/Grooming	100	• Relaxation	• Improved health • Increased social standing
Exercise	50	• Relaxation • Satisfaction • Enjoyment • Social Interaction	• Improved health • Improved athletic performance
Texting/Talking on Phone	50	• Enjoyment • Social Interaction	• Better relationships with friends
Checking e-mail/ Web Surfing	80	• Enjoyment • Relaxation • Social Interaction	
Practicing Flute	20	• Satisfaction • Enjoyment	• Improved technique • Increased possibility of admission to music school • Increased possibility of music scholarship • Less fighting with parents
Eating	20	• Enjoyment • Social Interaction • Relaxation	• Improved health
Studying	20	• Satisfaction	• Improved grades • Increased chance of scholarship • Less stress • Less fighting with parents
Household Chores	20	• Satisfaction	• Less fighting with parents • Develops responsibilities

The "Activities and Benefits Worksheet" can show patterns in how you spend your time. In the example worksheet, the student invests more time in activities that provide enjoyment, social interaction, and relaxation than in those that provide short-term satisfaction and significant long-term gains.

Tip 10: Make a priority list.

Once you have used the "Activity Journal" and the "Activities and Benefits Worksheet" to identify how you spend your time, you can start making decisions about how much value you place on each task.

Index cards are useful when prioritizing your activities because they can be spread out, reordered, and stored easily. On the front of an index card, write the name of one of the activities you listed in your "Activity Journal." Draw a line down the middle of the card's back. On the left-hand side of the card, list the short-term benefits you identified on the "Activities and Benefits Worksheet." Write the long-term benefits on the right-hand side. Use a new index card for each activity. Your activity cards should look something like this:

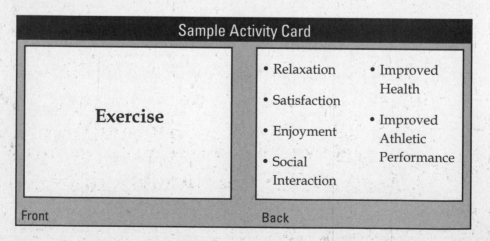

Sample Activity Card

Exercise

- Relaxation
- Satisfaction
- Enjoyment
- Social Interaction

- Improved Health
- Improved Athletic Performance

Front   Back

Once your cards are complete, lay them face down on your desk, table, or floor. Fold each card in half so that you can only see the list of long-term benefits. You may need to use paperclips to keep the cards folded. Arrange the cards in a line so that they activity that offers the most important long-term benefits is first and those that offer few or no long-term benefits are last.

Bear in mind that everybody has different priorities. A student who is interested in a career as a professional athlete or is counting on an athletic scholarship may value the long-term benefits of exercise more than the benefits of practicing flute. A student who is determined to major in music will have different priorities. Base your decisions on what you want from your life, not on what you think your parents, teachers, or friends want you to value.

After you are satisfied with the order of the activities based on the long-term benefits, flip the folded cards over so that the short-term benefits show. Be careful not to change the position of the cards. You may decide to rearrange the cards based on the short-term benefits, but avoid moving a card more than one or two positions.

Next unfold the cards and turn them over so you can see the activity name. Fine tune the order by switching adjacent cards. Write down the final order of the cards, starting with the most important activity and ending with the activity with the least benefits. This is your priority list. Complete highest-priority tasks before engaging in lower-priority activities.

It may not be necessary to cut out activities with few long-term benefits completely. Sometimes, just cutting back on an activity can free up time. In the example "Activity Journal," by halving the time spent on television and the Internet, the student will have over an hour and a half more time in the average day.

Wrap a rubber band around your deck of activity cards or store them in a card file box. Good time managers review their schedules regularly. If your responsibilities, hobbies, or study requirements change, you may need to use your cards again to reprioritize your activities.

Tip 11: Use technology.

Modern conveniences can help you watch your favorite television shows, research papers, and stay in touch with friends and family on your own schedule. Modern technology can also help with time management.

You can record your favorite shows on videocassettes or DVD-R. By having shows you want to watch available, you will not waste time mindlessly flipping through channels.

Instead of making multiple calls or writing several e-mails to spread news, use a social networking Web site or personal blog to stay in touch with friends and family. Be aware that for some people, these sites can be significant time drainers. You may need to set limits on how long you allow yourself to check friends' sites and update your own.

Your local or school library may allow you to search their holdings from their Web sites. This allows you to find and request the books and magazines you need from your home computer. If this feature is available to you, use it to start researching papers and projects even if your library is closed.

Record lists of vocabulary words, dates, definitions, and other facts you need to memorize. Play the information back on your MP3 players or tape recorder while you exercise or commute.

Know when to put the electronic toys away. If your handheld computer or cellular phone is a distraction, turn it off until you complete a task.

Tip 12: Make study time convenient.

If you are reading this book, you almost certainly rated studying as a high priority in the previous exercise. Remember that good time managers complete high-priority tasks before moving on to other activities.

Odds are that you identified several lower-priority activities that are more fun than studying. You would most likely prefer to do them than to sit down with your textbooks. Humans tend to find excuses not to do things if there are too many barriers, especially if there are more enjoyable ways to spend their time. If you anticipate the obstacles to a successful study session and take preemptive measures to overcome them, you have a better chance of not having your efforts sidelines by temptation. There are several reasons you may find it easy to postpone your study session or skip it altogether.

You are hungry. It is hard to stay motivated through a growling stomach and low blood sugar.

People are waiting on you. If your friends are waiting for you to learn your French vocabulary list before they can leave for a movie, you might feel pressured to cut your study session short.

You are tired. If you wait to study until after a 10-mile run or a double shift at work, you may not have enough energy left.

There is too much fun going on around you. If the rest of your family is enjoying pizza and a movie while you study chemistry, you may feel left out and resentful.

You are short on time. If you have to leave for a football game in 10 minutes, you may feel too rushed to complete your assignment to the best of your ability.

You are physically uncomfortable. It is difficult to concentrate if you are too warm, too cold, or sitting in a position that hurts.

You feel pressured by another task. If you dread working on your English paper, you may not be able to focus on you algebra homework.

Try to schedule your study time so that you minimize these barriers. To avoid the situations like the ones above, you may find it helpful to:

- Have a snack before you start studying.

- Keep single-serving snacks and drinks in your room to enjoy during study breaks.

- Arrange to study in the library after school.

- Take a 10- to 15-minute nap after work or practice before you open the books.

- Review your personal and work schedule before you set a time to study.

- Wear layers or bring a sweater with you when you study.

- Choose a study location that has plenty of light and comfortable chairs.

- If you feel pressured by the short amount of time you have available to work on a particular assignment, review your daily "to do" list and see if there is anything that would fit into the time window better.

- Tackle difficult tasks first. If a difficult or boring assignment is hanging over your head, work on it first. Even if you do not complete the task, you may be able to concentrate on your other work better if you have made progress on the activity you dread.

Think of all the excuses you have used in the past to cut your study sessions short or to skip them altogether. Try to find ways to prevent those barriers from occurring in the future. Make studying as easy and comfortable as possible.

Case Study: Thomas Stover

Thomas Stover

High School Student

I enjoy woodcarving, woodworking, listening to music, identifying trees and different types of woods, taking walks with my dog, riding dirt bikes, and hiking in forests.

The first thing I do when I get home from school is my homework. That way, I do not have to worry about it all day and night. I also take every chance I get in school to do my homework so I do not have to do it when I am at home and have more enjoyable things to do.

Tip 13: Set time management goals.

Effective time management comes easily to some people. Others find it difficult to finish their high-priority tasks each day no matter how much time they have available.

Like studying, time management is a skill that can be learned and improved. One way to develop your time-management abilities is to set intermediate goals and work toward one for a few minutes each day.

Your time-management goals may include:

- Completing the "Activity Journal," "Activities and Benefits Worksheet," and priority cards exercises described in this chapter

- Reducing the amount of time spent on low-priority activities for a month

- Completing all high-priority activities every day for a week

- Studying in 15-minute chunks with five-minute breaks every day for a week

- Updating and using your "to-do" list every day for a month

- Consulting your yearly calendar every day for a month

Write your goal on your calendar, your planner, or a sheet of paper that you can keep handy. Use a simple chart to keep track of your progress. After you complete a milestone, reward yourself and start working toward a new goal. Some possible rewards to keep you polishing your time-management skills include:

- A watch, timer, or clock

- An interesting tea or coffee to enjoy during your breaks

- An extra 15 minutes to indulge in your favorite low-priority activity

- A new notebook or pen

Use short-term goals and rewards to keep yourself motivated and excited about developing your time-management skills.

Tip 14: Schedule downtime.

No matter how intensive your academic schedule, you do not need to devote every free minute to studying. Setting aside some time to relax and have fun can help you approach problems more creatively, have more energy to complete your assignments, and maintain your physical health.

Athletes who do not rest well after hard workouts may become "overtrained." Overtraining occurs when muscles and joints are exercised past the point needed for optimal improvement. Overtrained athletes are more susceptible to injury, illness, and burnout.

Students who do not have enough time to rest and enjoy non-academic pursuits may have symptoms similar to overtrained athletes. Signs that you may be working too much include:

- Irritability
- Frequent illness

- Inability to focus
- Loss of appetite

- Insomnia

- Difficulty waking up in the morning

- Reduced enthusiasm for subjects you used to enjoy

- Constant sluggishness or tiredness

If you have any of these symptoms, you may need to revise your study schedule to allow for more down time. These signs indicate that your body is under stress. Your family doctor can help you determine whether or not the cause is overwork.

Try to fit down time into your schedule before you feel overwhelmed or exhausted. Make room for some fun activities, especially during high stress periods such as final exams. Even 15 minutes engaged in a relaxing activity can help rejuvenate you and allow you to study more efficiently.

During down time you may enjoy activities like:

- Meditating
- Writing in a journal

- Napping
- Daydreaming

- Playing a board game
- Chatting with friends

- Taking a walk
- Listening to music

- Working on a hobby
- Exercising

- Drawing or painting
- Playing a video game

- Watching a television show
- Cooking

📚   Reading a novel or magazine

Avoid starting activities that you have trouble stopping, leave you feeling tense, or sap your energy. Try to find an activity that will leave you refreshed and eager to return to work.

Look for an activity that will reduce your workload, not add to it. For some students, a run around the neighborhood park can help clear their minds and help them focus on their assignments. Other students may feel obsessed over their speed and feel the constant need to improve. For them, the same run may become another source of stress. Do not be afraid to try out different down time activities. Seek out new ways to give yourself a break.

Tip 15: Leave yourself some wiggle room.

Do not structure your day so tightly that there is not room for the unexpected. Leave some extra time to work on that geometry proof that seems impossible, watch the extra innings of the softball game, or talk with a friend who is going through a crisis. There are many different ways to help prevent having your schedule derailed by unexpected events.

Try to overestimate the amount of time it will take to complete a task. Do not build your schedule around the best-case scenario.

Start important tasks as early in the day as possible. If you leave them until last, you may find that you do not have enough time available to complete them to the best of your ability.

Think about alternative activities that reach the same goals. If a traffic jam is preventing you from going home to study German, try to recite your vocabulary words or practice verb conjugations while you sit in your car. Instead of trying to wait out the weather to take your evening run, exercise to a video inside.

Always be prepared to study. Keep a notebook or study guide in your purse or jacket pocket. If you have a longer than expected wait at the doctor's office, use the time to review the material.

If a task takes less time than you anticipated, do not use the extra time to watch television or play a video game. Instead, use the extra minutes you had allotted to get a jump on other work you have scheduled.

Schedule down time. If needed, you can use some or all of your relaxation time to finish unexpectedly long or difficult assignments. Remember from the previous tip that down time is an important component to an effective study habit. Do not make a habit of cutting your down time short.

Leaving just enough time to finish each task can increase your stress and cause time-management issues if one activity runs long. Studying is not a sprint, it is a marathon. Remember that steady, consistent progress is more likely to help you reach your goals than hard bursts of intense work. Trying to compress too many jobs into the time you have will make you more susceptible to overtraining symptoms and burnout.

FIND YOUR
LEARNING STYLE

Even after learning to prioritize activities and set aside time to study, some students still do not seem to have enough time to master material and improve their grades. The problem with these students might be how they study, not how much they study.

TYPES OF LEARNERS

There are many techniques that can help high school students study more efficiently. One student may learn best through flashcards. Another may prefer to listen to taped class notes. To find the techniques that are likely to work best for you, think about how you have learned best in the past.

Learning styles can be divided into three broad groups: auditory learners, visual learners, and tactile or kinesthetic learners.

Auditory Learners

Auditory learners find that they process information better if they hear it. They often prefer to have a teacher describe how to complete an assignment instead of reading the directions.

Visual Learners

Visual learners learn more from seeing information presented. Visual learners may retain more information if they see it in a chart or diagram. During a lecture, they may have to form a mental image of a process or concept in their heads before they can understand it.

Tactile/Kinesthetic Learners

Tactile learners learn more by doing than by hearing or seeing. They may prefer to jump straight into a task and learn from their mistakes rather than following a flow chart or verbal directions.

CREATING YOUR PERSONAL LEARNING PLAN

By creating a study plan around your learning style, you can maximize the amount you learn in a minimal amount of time.

Tip 16: Define your learning style.

Take a test, designed for determining what kind of learner you are. Use the one on the following page, or find a different test to take. After taking the test, visit your school counselor for further assessments.

The first step in creating a personal learning plan is to determine what kind of learner you are. The following exercise can help you decide if you would benefit more from auditory, visual, or tactile learning techniques.

What Type of Learner Are You?

Directions: Circle the number that corresponds to how well each of the statements describes you.

1 = This statement does not describe me at all.

2 = This statement somewhat describes me.

3 = This statement describes me exceptionally well.

1. When I read my textbook, I tend to skip to the diagrams and highlighted sections.	1	2	3
2. I like to have a written list to follow when solving math problems.	1	2	3
3. In my free time, I prefer to draw than to listen to music.	1	2	3
4. I would rather write a play than act in one.	1	2	3
5. I find it hard to study if other people are around, even if they are being quiet.	1	2	3
Add your answers for statements one through five. This is your Visual Learning Score (VLS).			
Your VLS:			
6. I usually learn spelling words by reciting them over and over.	1	2	3
7. I learn more from lectures than from reading the textbook.	1	2	3
8. I remember song lyrics easily.	1	2	3
9. I like to debate issues.	1	2	3
10. I find it hard to study in loud places.	1	2	3
Add your answers for statements six through ten. This is your Auditory Learning Score (ALS).			
Your ALS:			
11. Experiments and demonstrations help me understand concepts.	1	2	3
12. I learn definitions best by writing them out several times.	1	2	3
13. I use my hands to explain science and math concepts.	1	2	3
14. Some of my best ideas come when I am being physically active.	1	2	3
15. I learn dances and athletic movements easily.	1	2	3
Add your answers for statements 11 through 15. This is your Tactile Learning Score (TLS).			
Your TLS:			

Compare your VLS, ALS, and TLS. The category with the highest score indicates your primary learning style. If two or three of your scores are similar, you may benefit from using study techniques that stimulate different senses.

Tip 17: Try new things.

Do not be afraid to try techniques recommended for people with other learning styles. Many students learn better by using several senses. Even if you are a primarily auditory learner, read over the tips for visual and tactile learners; try a few out. You may find that you understand the concepts more clearly or are able to recall the information better for the next test.

Tip 18: Auditory learners: Recite and repeat.

Auditory learners tend to understand and remember better if they are able to hear the information. If you are an auditory learner, the following techniques may help you learn more efficiently.

Read information out loud. Study in a place where you can make a little noise without bothering other people. Read your textbook, assignments, and notes aloud. Try to speak conversationally instead of robotically. If you need to memorize a list of information, you may benefit by reading it aloud several times.

Tape your lectures. Being able to review verbal explanations and directions later, as you study, may help you understand complicated concepts. Make sure you have your teacher's permission before you record.

Quiz yourself. Ask yourself questions as you study. Try to explain information in your own words.

Talk about your studies. Tell your friends and family about the more interesting points you have learned. The more you talk about a subject, the better it will become cemented in your long-term memory.

Auditory learning techniques are well-suited for memorizing foreign language vocabulary lists, learning definitions in all subjects, understanding sequences in math and science, and internalizing lists of facts.

Tip 19: Visual learners: Sketch out concepts.

Visual learners learn most efficiently when they can organize information in a chart, illustration, or diagram. If you are a visual learner, the following strategies may help you.

Look for information parallels and use them to make comparison tables. For example, if you are studying physiology, you could make a chart that lists the purpose, location, and shape for each bone you are learning about. To help understand an assigned reading about poetry, you could use the information to make a chart for the arrangement of syllables, number of feet, common uses, and examples of iambic pentameter, trochaic tetrameter, anapestic trimeter, and dactylic hexameter. The information on comparison tables can often be used to answer "compare and contrast" questions on exams or assignments.

Copy graphs, charts, and figures. For instance, if your textbook uses a figure to help explain a concept that your teacher lectured about, copy the figure in your class notes.

Use drawings to help you internalize foreign language word lists. If you are learning the parts of the body in Spanish, draw or trace a person and label each part with the corresponding term. If you are learning household nouns, sketch a simple room and label the furnishings.

Make flow charts to show cycles, processes, and cause-and-effect relationships. Flow charts are a way to translate written information into a visual format. When constructing a flow chart, different shapes are used to show how the data relates. The shapes used in flow charts are listed in the chart below.

Flow Chart Structures			
Shape	**Physical Description**	**Name**	**Type of Information Enclosed**
	Rectangle with short ends rounded	Terminator	The state of the system at the beginning and end of the chart
	Rectangle with short ends slanted	Input or Output	Information that is added to the system (input) or that is the result of the system (output)
	Rectangle	Process	Actions that happen
	Diamond	Decision	A question asked about the system

Flow charts can be used to illustrate scientific processes, how to solve mathematical problems, causes and effects in historical scenarios, and plots of stories and novels.

A science textbook might include the following description of the nitrogen cycle.

The Nitrogen Cycle

Bacteria convert nitrogen from the air into a form that plants can use. This process, called "nitrogen fixation," changes N2 to nitrate or ammonium ions. If nitrogen is available as nitrate, plants must first convert the nitrate to nitrite ions and then to ammonium ions. These ammonium ions are used to make organic compounds such as chlorophyll, genetic building blocks, and amino acids. This process is called "assimilation."

As dead plants and animals decompose, they release an organic form of nitrogen. "Ammonification" occurs when bacteria convert the organic material into ammonia. Different bacteria can convert the ammonia to nitrates ("nitrification"). Other species of bacteria process the nitrates to release N2 back into the atmosphere in a process termed "denitrification."

Some students will understand and remember this information better by constructing a comparison table.

Nitrogen Cycle Process				
Process Name	**Input**	**Intermediaries**	**Output**	**Performed By**
Nitrogen fixation	N_2 from the air		Nitrate, ammonium ions	Bacteria
Assimilation	Nitrate	Nitrite ions, ammonium ions	Chlorophyll, genetic building blocks, amino acids	Plants
Ammonification	Organic nitrogen		Ammonia	Bacteria
Nitrification	Ammonia		Nitrates	Bacteria
Denitrification	Nitrates		N_2	Bacteria

A comparison table can help you understand and remember material, and it can make it easier to find the information you need to answer questions about the reading. A study guide to help prepare a student for a test on the nitrogen cycle might include questions like:

> ☙   How many processes are in the nitrogen cycle?

> ☙   Which processes are performed by bacteria?

> ☙   How are plants involved in the nitrogen cycle?

> ☙   What forms of nitrogen can plants use?

For visual learners, the answers to these questions are easier to find in the comparison table than in the text.

The nitrogen cycle reading can also be translated into a flow chart.

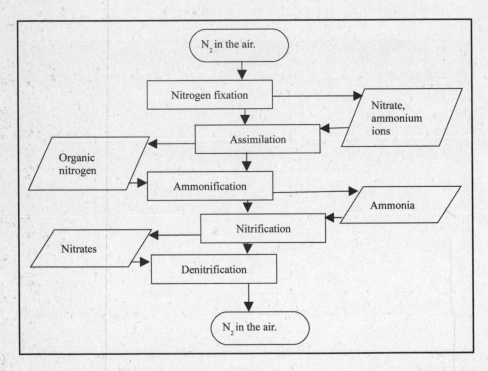

Like the comparison table, the flow chart can make it easier to answer certain questions, such as:

- Why is the process called a cycle?

- How is assimilation related to ammonification?

- What do assimilation and denitrification have in common?

It may be helpful to translate a single piece of written information into several visual interpretations. The more ways visual learners see the information, the more likely they are to remember it.

If you find the lines on your notebook paper distracting when you construct a diagram, flow chart, or comparison table in your notebook, use unlined paper. If you feel frustrated because the visual representations you draw look sloppy, consider using a computer. Most word-processing software packages include tools to help you make and edit charts and tables. If you have trouble drawing, simple clip-art pictures can be used to illustrate vocabulary words. If you do not have access to a computer, you may prefer to trace pictures from magazines, your textbook, or coloring books. If you reproduce someone else's art, respect copyright laws and keep the diagram only for personal use.

Tip 20: Tactile learners: Let your fingers help you learn.

Tactile learners learn more by touching and experimenting with an object than by hearing or reading about it. At first, it may seem difficult to incorporate tactile learning techniques into subjects traditionally taught through lectures or reading. Although, with some creativity, tactile learners can find opportunities for hands-on studying throughout their curriculum.

If you are a tactile learner, you may benefit from some targeted changes to your study habits, such as the following.

- Tactile learners tend to think more clearly during or after exercise. Use this trait to your advantage by incorporating five minutes of stretching, weight lifting, or aerobic activity during each of your study breaks.

- When reading textbooks, use your fingers to trace out cycles and diagrams.

- If you have a laboratory exercise during class, take notes about what you did. When you study, try to replay the experience and reflect on what the results mean.

- If you are studying a foreign language, purchase some models of the nouns you need to learn or make your own models out of clay. Label the models with the foreign words or phrases. Review your vocabulary by picking up the model and handling it while you say the word. Use removable labels so you can quiz yourself with the models later.

- Use pennies, cards, blocks, or paperclips to work out or check math problems.

- Ask your teacher for examples of physical applications of math or science equations.

- For many tactile learners, the key to efficient studying is interactivity. Study guides with flaps and folds are easy to make and can help you understand concepts and remember facts. These interactive tools can be customized depending on the subject and type of information you need to learn.

FLAP BOOKS

If you need to review a list of vocabulary words, definitions, or facts, fold a sheet of card stock in half to make a long rectangle. Cut the folded paper into appropriately sized sections, but stop each cut about a centimeter before the fold. This will make a row of connected cards. On the outside of each card, write the word, name, or date. Inside the card, write the definition or importance of that term. Study by reading the outside of a card, then lifting the flap and reviewing the information inside.

If you are going to use your study guide for several days, only have notebook or copier paper available, or plan to take it to school with you, you may prefer to cut only the top fold and leave the bottom fold in one piece. This will make a sturdier study guide.

If you have to learn more terms than you can fit using a single sheet of paper, make additional flap books or use all three unfolded sides of a manila folder. You can even recycle used manila folders. If there are marks on the folder, simply write the terms and explanations on small pieces of paper and glue them to the flaps.

SLIDE CARDS

A slide card is an interactive study tool that allows you to learn the properties of one or more items, people, or historical eras.

You will need two pieces of notebook or copier paper to make a simple slide card. Fold the first sheet of paper widthwise (short sides together). Fold the second sheet of paper lengthwise (long sides together). The information you want to study goes on the second sheet of paper. Arrange the information in a table.

Each column corresponds to a property. Each row will contain information about a single item, person, or time period. Try to keep each row about the same size.

On your first sheet of fold paper, mark off a window that is the same size as a row of information on your long sheet. Carefully cut out the window. Fit the long sheet between the folds of the first sheet. Check to make sure the information matches up with the window. Remove the information sheet. On the sheet with the window, staple together the edges opposite the fold. Be sure to leave enough room between the staples and the fold for the information sheet to slide easily.

Insert the information sheet between the staples and the fold of the first paper. Label the window to show what information is in each column. Slide the information sheet up and down to reveal each row. You can get fancy and add a flap to hide some of the columns so that you can quiz yourself. Alternatively, you can cover parts of the entry with your hand.

Tip 21: Become the teacher.

Whether you are a visual, auditory, or tactile learner, you can remember material faster and more thoroughly if you take on a teaching role. Once you understand a difficult concept, explain it to someone else. Your student may be a classmate, parent, or sibling. Present the method in several ways using techniques from each learning style. Try to answer any questions your student has. If you cannot answer a question, it may reflect a hole in your understanding. Attempt to go through the material without consulting your notes. Jot down points you had trouble remembering and study those areas more thoroughly.

Teaching someone else material can help reinforce facts and concepts. To get the most out of the experience, keep the following hints in mind.

Be patient with your pupil. Try not to show your frustration if you cannot explain the material in a way that helps him or her understand it.

Be prepared. The experience is not likely to be enjoyable for you or your volunteer student if you have to keep running out of the room to look up a fact or get a chart. Respect your pupil's time.

Remember the reason. Do not go off on a tangent that is unrelated to the material you are trying to teach. Save the discussions and debates for after your study session.

Look your pupil in the eye. Eye contact will help engage your students and let you assess how well they understand your explanations.

Case Study: Elizabeth Bannister

Elizabeth Bannister

High School Student

Sometimes just making flashcards is sufficient, but if you need more help then you have them to give you a hand in memorization work. Group study rarely works. It is too easy to get distracted. Do not put study time off.

Study well ahead of time and then you just have to review a bit beforehand. If you pay attention in class, you do not have to study as much. Do not highlight everything. Only highlight what is really important and what you do not already know.

CREATE YOUR STUDY SPACE

O nce you have the time to study and a few techniques to help you learn more efficiently, you should start perfecting your study area.

Having a designated study space will help you manage your time better. You will not have to clear the kitchen table to have enough room to work, or root through the closet to find a lamp. A good study space is one that is available to support your learning whenever you need it.

There are a few things that are necessary to include in a good study space. At a minimum, your study space should include:

- A chair
- A clock or timer
- A flat surface large enough to hold an open textbook and a notebook
- A drawer, bin, or basket to organize pencils, pens, rulers, and other small tools

≋   A wastepaper basket

In addition, you may find it helpful to include the following in your workspace:

≋   A bookcase   ≋   A file cabinet

≋   A corkboard   ≋   A lamp

≋   A footrest

Where you build your study space depends on your preferences and what you have available. A desk or table in your bedroom, the corner of the family room, or even the laundry room can be the starting point for a work area. If you do not have a desk or table, a useful work area can be constructed by resting a smooth, sturdy piece of wood between two small file cabinets. Your study area should be a quiet place, relatively free from distractions.

If you do not have a place to set aside for studying, or if you study in a public place such as a library, see Tip 26 for information about creating a mobile study kit.

Tip 22: Do not worry about getting your space perfect right way.

You may not have a tidy, organized work area available immediately. Do not reduce your study time to prepare your space. Instead, schedule a block of time to work on your work area every day. Even if you only have five minutes to devote to the task, over the course of several days you will have made significant progress toward creating an appropriate area.

Do not use an untidy or incomplete work area as an excuse not to study, and do not get so concerned about the decor of your space that it interferes with your work.

Tip 23: Protect your body.

If your study area is poorly equipped, you may finish your study session fatigued or in pain. If you sit in an awkward position for extended periods of time, you will increase your risk of developing musculoskeletal disorders (MSD) including muscle and joint strain, pinched nerves, and pulled tendons.

There are different signs and symptoms that could indicate that your study area is negatively affecting your health. Your work area may be interfering with your health if you experience any of the following signs:

- Dry, itchy, or sore eyes
- Muscle cramps
- Numbness in your hands
- Blurred or double vision
- Muscle weakness
- Swollen joints
- Loss of mobility or stiffness in your joints
- Localized pain anywhere in your body

If you have these symptoms, check with your family doctor to rule out a more serious health problem. If the cause is your studying environment, some simple choices can help you work more comfortably and protect your body from physical stress.

LIGHTING

Unless your study area is in a particularly well-lit room, you will want a lamp to help you see your work better and reduce eye fatigue. Even if your work area receives ample sunlight during the day, a lamp may be useful during nighttime study sessions or bad weather.

If you have a small writing surface, you may prefer a small lamp that can be stored in a drawer until needed. Clip-on lamps are adjustable, have a small footprint, and are often less expensive than desk lamps. Gooseneck lamps also take up less room than traditional desk lamps and can be adjusted to direct light where you need it.

Desk

Your desk or study table should be high enough that it does not pinch or restrict movement of your legs. The height should allow you to keep you wrists, hands, and forearms parallel to the floor, but not so high that your shoulders are strained. The edge of the desk should be rounded or padded to protect your forearms.

Chair

Try to find a chair that adjusts to let you work in different positions. This will help you stay comfortable throughout a long study session and reduce physical fatigue. The seat of your chair should be comfortable. The edge of the seat should not cut into your thighs. The height should allow your feet to rest on the ground while your forearms and thighs stay parallel to the ground. If you need a high chair to keep your arms and wrists comfortable when working at your desk, consider using a footrest to keep your legs from dangling. The backrest should support your spine and not force it into an awkward position.

COMPUTER

If you use a computer in your work area, make sure the monitor is at least 20 inches from your face. Lights should not be too bright or positioned directly at the monitor. Your keyboard should be positioned so that you can keep your wrists and arms in a neutral position while you type.

GENERAL ERGONOMIC PRINCIPLES

When furnishing your work area, keep the following guidelines in mind:

- Your hands, wrists, forearms, thighs, and hips should all be parallel to the floor as you work.

- Your shoulders, upper arms, and knees should be relaxed at all times.

- Your feet and back should be fully supported.

- Your elbows should remain close to your body.

- Change your position throughout your work session.

- Any piece of furniture that presses against your body should be rounded or padded.

Tip 24: Identify your distractions.

If you find yourself staring at the photographs on your desk or singing along with the music from your radio instead of focusing on your English homework, your work area may be sabotaging your ability to study efficiently.

To free your work area of distractions, you must identify what elements in your environment are keeping you from paying close attention to your work. Some common distractions are listed below. During your next study session, decide if you would be able to get more accomplished if you removed them.

MUSIC

Some students claim they study better when music is playing in the background. On the other hand, because their attention is spread between the music and their work, they are unable to focus properly on either. This may make a study session more fun, it also makes it less efficient. If your schedule allows for a leisurely study session, this might not be an issue. If you want to minimize the time you spend at your desk, turn off the radio.

DECORATIONS

An attractive work area can help make the time you spend studying more enjoyable and comfortable. If you enjoy the view from your chair, sitting down at your desk will not feel like such a chore. Conversely, some students are unable to resist playing with the toys on their windowsills or gazing at the optical illusion posters on their walls.

If you find the decorations in your work area a little too appealing, put them out of sight and out of reach.

COMPUTERS

Your computer can be a useful research and presentation tool. It can also be extremely entertaining. For some students, a five-minute break to play a video game or check e-mail can stretch into 30 minutes of wasted study time. When you are at the computer, you may feel and look like you are working no matter how little you accomplish.

If you find that your computer is more distracting than it is helpful, study on the opposite side of the room from the computer or in a different room entirely. If it is not possible to set up separate work areas, commit to keeping the computer turned off unless it is absolutely needed.

TELEPHONE

A constantly ringing telephone can break your concentration and waste time. If possible, turn the telephone's ringer off while you study. If your friends, family, or employers need to be able to contact you, make sure they know your study schedule and respect the rule that the telephone is for emergencies only.

PETS

It can be hard to concentrate on calculus when your cat insists on sitting on your notebook and your dog keeps howling at the traffic outside. Secure attention-seeking animals in another room when you study, and be sure to give them some extra scratches behind the ear when you finish your work.

PARENTS

Your parents may be sabotaging your study session with constant interruptions. Reminders to complete chores, complaints about the car's empty gas tank, and even well-meaning suggestions to have a snack can break your train of thought and keep you from studying effectively and efficiently.

Honesty and calmness are regularly your best tools when faced with a disruptive parent. Talk with your parents about your studying goals and why your study time is important to you. You will most likely have better luck if you initiate this talk before the situation escalates into a yelling match. If your parent consistently interrupts your studies to have you take out the trash, feed the dog, or wash the dishes, discuss the possibility of completing your chores before you begin studying or deferring them until after your schoolwork is finished.

Tip 25: Keep your supplies and resources handy.

Your study area should be stocked with all the tools you regularly use while studying. Supplies are objects you use and need to replace periodically. Resources are tools that can be used many times and do not need to be replaced unless they break or become outdated. Supplies you may need to stock include:

- pens
- notebook paper
- permanent markers
- extra notebook
- paint
- staples
- highlighters
- tape

- pencils
- coloring pencils
- eraser
- copier paper
- report covers
- pocket folders
- lead/ink refills
- correction fluid

- index cards
- paperclips
- construction paper
- adhesive labels

In addition, you may find the following resources useful as you work:

- dictionary
- thesaurus
- calculator
- writing style manual
- atlas
- pencil sharpener
- stapler
- three-hole punch
- ruler
- French curve
- protractor
- compass
- paint brushes
- scissors
- foreign language dictionaries

It is unlikely that you will have to purchase all these supplies and resources at once. Use what you have on hand to get started and build up your tool collection as you need and can afford to purchase more. You do not need to go overboard when stocking your study area. There are many ways to save money and still have the tools you need.

- Buy supplies in bulk from an office supply or discount store.
- Take advantage of "back-to-school" sales to stock up on tools you know you will need.

❧ Used books and equipment can be just as useful as, and much less expensive than, new ones. Check online retailers and auction sites, local consignment shops, and thrift stores to see if they have what you need.

❧ Ask your teachers if they have any resources or supplies that past students may have left or donated.

❧ Look for reference materials such as atlases and dictionaries at library book sales.

❧ Add the supplies and resources you need to your birthday or holiday gift wish list.

You will waste time and energy if you need to walk into another room or rummage through a messy drawer to find the tool you need. The following hints can help you keep your supplies and resources organized and ready to use.

❧ Use plastic dividers to separate large drawers into several spaces. This will help prevent small supplies from falling to the bottom of the drawer.

❧ Create drawers for your bookcase using baskets or bins.

❧ Keep frequently used supplies like pencils and erasers in a cup or tray on top of your work surface.

❧ Use recloseable plastic bags to keep small supplies like index cards and paperclips from getting lost in your drawers.

❧ If you buy supplies in bulk, keep only what you need in your desk. Save space in your work area by storing the surplus in a separate box or in a closet.

Tip 26: Do not use the lack of a dedicated study space as an excuse.

If you do not have a desk, room, or corner that you can use as a study area, a mobile study kit lets your stay organized as you study.

No matter where you need to work, you may need to include the following in your portable study kit.

Pencils, pens, and erasers: You will need something to write with to take notes and complete written assignments.

Pencil lead or ink refills: Avoid the frustration of having plenty of pencils, but nothing to write with.

Calculator: Even if you are not studying math, a calculator can come in handy to figure out how an assignment will influence your final grade in a class or to work with numerical data or figures in any subject.

Scissors: If you like to make flap books or slide cards, a pair of scissors is indispensable. Small safety or blunt nose scissors are sufficient for most tasks, will take up less room in your kit, and will be less likely to poke a hole in your bag.

Ruler: Even a compact four-inch ruler is handy for taking measurements or drawing lines for visual and tactile learning tools.

Index cards: An index card can function as a bookmark, "to-do" list, or flashcard.

Paperclips: A paperclip can be used to organize handouts or mark pages in a book.

Small pencil sharpener: Even if you are studying in a room with a public sharpener, having your own is more convenient.

These small tools tend to fall to the bottom of backpacks and tote boxes. If you store these supplies in a zippered bag, plastic pencil box, or small section of a larger bag, they will be easier to find when you need them.

The subjects you are plan to work on and the assignments you need to complete will define other resources that will need to go in your study kit. These may include:

Laptop computer: You may need word processing capabilities to work on a paper, a spreadsheet program to complete a business math assignment, or publishing software to finish a slideshow for a presentation.

Mobile storage device: If you do not have a laptop computer and are going to work in a facility that has a computer you can use, then a rewritable CD, memory card, or thumb drive will allow you to transport your files between workstations.

Textbooks: You may need to bring some of your textbooks with you to complete an assignment, read, or serve as a reference.

Notebooks: When completing an assignment, you may want to refer to previous work or information that was presented in class.

Art supplies: If you are working on a presentation or art project, pack and bring all the tools you think you will need.

Paper: In addition to lined notebook paper, consider bringing copy or construction paper to make flap books and slide cards.

Reference books: If you are studying a foreign language, bring the appropriate dictionaries. If you are writing an essay on a novel, make sure you have a copy of the book with you.

Compass and protractor: Algebra, geometry, and trigonometry students in particular should keep these handy.

Depending on where you plan on holding your study sessions, you may need to stock your kit with additional tools.

The Library

School or public libraries are the study areas of choice for some students. They are more often than not quiet and stocked with dictionaries, thesauri, and other reference tools you may need. You will almost certainly find a desk or table to work on, but the lighting may be insufficient for close-up work. A battery powered lamp can help prevent eye strain and let you study more comfortably. If the chairs and tables are uncomfortable, consider bringing a foot rest or seat cushion.

A Friend's House

Working with a friend can give you a chance to talk through difficult concepts and quiz each other. The tools you need to take will depend on your friend's work area. If your friend's work area is organized and well-equipped, your basic study kit and the textbooks and notes you need for specific subjects may be enough. During your first few study sessions at your friend's house, make a list of what addition resources you need to bring.

A COMMON AREA IN YOUR HOME

You may need to set up a temporary study area each night on the kitchen table, your parent's desk, or a sibling's craft table. Although this may seem like an inconvenience, this setup can offer several benefits. Since you need to clear your materials away after your study session, you will have more opportunity to keep your materials organized. Because you are unlikely to have to move your study kit more than a few yards, you can pack it with useful tools that would be too heavy to lug to the library, including:

Coloring pencils: The diagrams and maps in your notes will be easier to read and understand if they are drawn in color.

Permanent markers: Permanent markers are useful for labeling notebooks and report covers.

Extra notebook: Keep a blank notebook on hand in case you fill one up, need one to organize a term paper or other large project, or left one in your locker.

Report covers: Presentation folders can keep your papers and large assignments organized and looking neat.

Stapler and staples: When studying for a test, you may find it helpful to staple related handouts, notes, and graded assignments together.

Pocket folders: If you prefer spiral bound notebooks to binders, pocket folders can help you keep class handouts organized and undamaged.

Highlighters: Coloring key words, dates, and names in your notes will help you review information quickly before a test.

Tape: A small piece of tape can repair torn handouts and damaged flap books.

Correction fluid: If you make a mistake that you can not erase, correction fluid can help you keep your notes and assignments neat.

Reference books: A dictionary, thesaurus, and style manual will help you write papers and essays that precisely reflect your ideas. In addition, an atlas can be helpful for history and social studies students.

Three-hole punch: If you keep your work organized in a binder, a three-hole punch will allow you to insert class handouts and graded tests.

PUBLIC PLACES

Students with busy after-school schedules may complete most of their studying at the gym, pool, dance studio, or break room. Although studying around your work, training, or rehearsal commitments can be a good use of your time, it may mean that you have to read, take notes, and complete assignments in a location that lacks a desk, chair, or adequate lighting. If you tend to study in public places, you may need to stock your study kit with some of the following items.

- **Writing surface:** If there are no desks available, a clipboard or smooth piece of wood will allow you to work on your lap or on the carpet.

- **Portable lamp:** Good lighting can help prevent eye fatigue and make your study session more pleasant. A battery-powered unit will free you from having to find a nearby outlet.

≋ **Pocket dictionary and thesaurus**

Multiple Places

If you need to work at the library on Tuesdays, the dance studio on Wednesdays, and the library on the weekends, you may need to prepare your kit to meet the needs of several different study environments. One possibility is to make a separate kit for each place you regularly study. Another alternative is to make a modular kit. For example, you might pack your basic tools in one small bag, your clipboard and portable lamp in another, and your reference books in the last. Depending on where you plan to study, you might bring one, two, or all three bags.

Packing Your Kit

There are many options available for storing and transporting your study kit. When choosing a case, take note what tools you will need to pack and how far you will have to carry the kit. Some choices to consider are:

≋ Backpack   ≋ Rolling luggage

≋ Tool box   ≋ Plastic crate or box

≋ Duffel or tote bag

A backpack distributes the weight of your tools over both shoulders while leaving your hands free. It is useful for carrying a light load for a long distance. If getting to your study area means a long walk with a large number of textbooks or reference materials, you might find a rolling suitcase less fatiguing. Art and technology students who need to carry many small, specialized tools such as paintbrushes or circuit boards may find a tool box or tackle box handy. Students who study in their home but do not have a permanent work area may prefer to keep their kit in a sturdy crate or box. If you need to transport oversized binders or books, a duffel, sports, or tote bag may be more convenient.

When selecting a case for your study kit, make sure that it is comfortable to move, even when loaded. Look for something that is sturdy enough to handle the weight of your books, equipment, and supplies. You may have a long and difficult walk home if the strap of your backpack breaks or the wheel of your suitcase falls off. If you will be taking your case outside, make sure it is waterproof.

Tip 27: Keep your workspace tidy.

It can be incredibly easy to let a study area slip into chaos. For many students, writing instruments, scrap paper, notes, spare change, and old soft drink cans tend to accumulate on their desks or tables despite their best intentions to keep the surface clean.

A messy work area can waste precious study time. Your study session should not be spent digging through a pile of papers to find your calculator, redoing your art history homework because it became lost in the clutter, or clearing off a few square inches of desk space to have enough room to write.

A cluttered study area is more than a time management issue. Important papers and supplies are more easily lost in a messy place. If you are unable to find the right tool you need to complete a task, you will not be able to do your best work. If you misplace a part of an assignment or a day's worth of notes, your grades may suffer.

The following tips can help you keep your work area tidy:

- Devote the last five minutes of every study session to putting away any supplies you used and clearing any clutter that has gathered in your study area.

- Keep often used tools in convenient locations. After you have used a tool, make sure to put it away.

- Do not keep your work surface clear by simply shoving stray papers in a drawer. Take time to straighten your drawers, too. Use shoeboxes or plastic drawer dividers to make compartments for all your supplies.

- Look for problem areas and make them unavailable if possible. If your wastepaper basket is always overflowing, get rid of it. If you have an ever-growing stack of papers on top of your file cabinet, but a lamp or decoration there instead.

- Reserve your study space for study tools. Do not store novels, sporting equipment, or hobby supplies in your work area.

Read Fast & Read Well

Whether you are a visual, tactile, or auditory learner, much of the information you are expected to learn will come in the form of the written word. In your English class, you may have to read novels, plays, short stories, essays, and grammar textbooks. When you study math, you may need to read and understand your textbook and word problems. Science students may need to read textbooks, lab manuals, articles, and lab reports. Music and art courses may include critiques and technique guides. Foreign language students may read about different cultures in addition to explanations about grammar rules.

When you read, you need to strike a balance between reading for content and reading for speed. When you read for content, you try to focus on every detail. Critical reading can be time consuming and tiring, but it is the best way to understand the material. When you read fast, you try to grasp the big picture of the material without spending much time on the nuances of the text.

Read the following passage twice, once for speed and then again for content. Each time, take notes about the material.

> Arboviruses are viral diseases that are carried by arthropods. The most common carriers of arboviruses are ticks and mosquitoes. Arbovirus symptoms may be limited to mild fevers and rashes, or they can cause paralysis and internal bleeding. Some arbovirus infections may result in death.
>
> Arboviruses occur throughout the world, and outbreaks of the diseases may be linked to weather patterns. For example, warm winters with high levels of precipitation followed by cold springs and unusually dry summers may increase the risk of a St. Louis encephalitis outbreak.
>
> Understanding environmental change can help scientists and healthcare practitioners predict and prepare for arboviral outbreaks and epidemics.

When you skimmed the material quickly, you may have picked up on the following main topics:

- Arboviruses are viral diseases carried by arthropods.

- Arbovirus outbreaks are linked to the environment.

When you reread the passage with a more critical eye, you might pick up the following additional information:

- Ticks and mosquitoes are the most common carriers of arboviruses.

- Weather patterns may influence arbovirus outbreaks.

- Cold springs, dry summers, and warm, wet summers may increase the risk of a St. Louis encephalitis outbreak.

One type of reading is not better than the other. There are times when it is more appropriate and time-conscious to read for speed, and other times when it will be more appropriate to take the time to read for content.

To study efficiently, it is important to be able to determine when it is best to read for content, read for speed, or find the right combination of the two extremes. When deciding how to read class material, consider a few questions.

How well do you currently understand the material? If you are already familiar with many of the concepts in the reading, you may be able to just skim the material and look for new information instead of reading each section intensely.

How much time do you have to read the material? If the only task on your daily "to do" list is reading a chapter in your history book, you can read the material closer than if you also need to complete a trigonometry assignment and learn a list of Spanish vocabulary words.

Why are you reading the material? If your goal for the session is to become familiar with the material that your teacher will cover in an upcoming lecture, a quick skim of the chapter may be sufficient. If you are trying to learn the material for an exam, you may need to spend more time on it in order to thoroughly understand the content.

How many more opportunities will you have to read the material? If you have several days to read the material, consider surveying it quickly first, then reading more critically later.

What type of material are you reading? It is difficult to follow the plot, characterization, and themes of a novel if you read for speed.

Tip 28: Use the features in your textbooks to help you read faster.

Textbooks tend to package important information so that it is easy to find. Your textbooks may have some of these features to help you study more efficiently:

- Chapter objectives

- Highlighted or boldface vocabulary words

- Definitions in boxes

- Chapter summaries

- Sidebar reviews of previously covered information

- Biographies of pivotal people

- Timelines

- Chapter outline

- Practice tests

- Examples

Taking a few minutes to become familiar with your textbook before you begin studying can help reduce your study time in the future. The book's introduction may explain the features and offer suggestions for studying the topic.

One way to read the material quickly is to pay attention only to information related to highlighted, bold, or underlined terms.

In the passage below, important terms are underlined. Read the passage quickly by just reading the underlined words and looking for their definitions. Take notes on what you read.

Computer networks can be set up in a variety of different configurations. When computers are linked in a circle with a single communication channel, the structure is called a ring. A ring is a slow but reliable configuration. A bus is similar to a ring configuration, but the network is linear, not circular. Like a ring, a bus network is slow but reliable.

In a mesh network, each computer is connected to every other computer in the organization. A mesh allows computers to transfer data to each other quickly, but it is a complex network. Adding a new node, or computer within the network, to a mesh structure can be complicated and time consuming.

When every computer in the network is linked to a single central computer, the structure is called a star. A star allows for quick data transfers, but can be risky. The safety of the entire network depends on the security and reliability of the central computer.

A hierarchy network resembles a pyramid. Each node is linked to several otherwise unlinked nodes. A hierarchy is more reliable than a star as the network can survive if a single computer fails. On the other hand, data transfer is relatively slow in a hierarchy system.

Different network structures can be combined to make a hybrid system. Hybrids are constructed using techniques that try to minimize the disadvantages of the component structures while maximizing the advantages.

Now, reread the passage carefully and slowly. Take notes on the information and compare to the notes from the first reading.

Example Notes for Reading for Speed Using Textbook Features and Reading Slowly for Content

Notes from Underlined Words	Notes from Entire Passage
• Ring: Computers are linked in a circle with a single communication channel.	Ring: Computers are linked in a circle with a single communication channel. Advantages: Reliable Disadvantages: Slow
• Bus: Computers are linked in a line with a single communication channel.	Bus: Computers are linked in a line with a single communication channel. Advantages: Reliable Disadvantages: Slow
• Mesh: Each computer is connected to every other computer in the network.	Mesh: Each computer is connected to every other computer in the network. Advantages: Quick Disadvantages: Complex
• Node: Computer within the network.	Node: Computer within the network.
• Star: Every computer in the network is linked to a single central computer.	Star: Every computer in the network is linked to a single central computer. Advantages: Quick Disadvantages: Risky
• Hierarchy: Network that resembles a pyramid or tree.	Hierarchy: Network that resembles a pyramid or tree. Advantages: Reliable Disadvantages: Slow
• Hybrid: Combination of tow or more different network structures.	Hybrid: Combination of two or more different network structures. Advantages: Depends on structures used and construction techniques. Disadvantages: Depends on structures used and construction techniques.

Although the quick reading of the underlined vocabulary words did not reveal every detail in the passage, it did provide a good overview of the main topics.

In math, science, and foreign language textbooks, it can be possible to get a quick overview of the material by reading only the examples. This works particularly well if the material has already been covered in class and you are only reading the textbook to review the concepts. If you rely on examples as your primary source for understanding the subject, you may be missing important explanations and exceptions.

Tip 29: Read the chapter objectives.

During most of your study sessions, you will almost certainly have to strike a balance between reading as quickly as possible and reading each word of every single paragraph. One way to read the material as thoroughly as possible during the time you have available is to skim over concepts that you already understand and spend more time reading information that is new to you.

If your textbook has a list of chapter objectives, use it to help you assess what you already know and on what sections your time would be more productively spent. Plan to spend more time reading the sections that correspond to concepts that confuse or seem unfamiliar to you.

Consider the following passage which lists possible objectives for a chapter in a geography textbook.

Chapter Objectives

After reading this chapter, you should be able to:

1. *List the states that comprise the Northeast region of the United States.*

2.   *Discuss the Northeast's role in the formation of the United States.*

3.   *Understand the current role of agriculture in the Northeast.*

4.   *Explain the historical importance of industrial papermaking in this region.*

5.   *Define and explain the importance of the Fundamental Orders.*

6.   *List the names and advancements made by Northeastern inventors in the 1800s.*

7.   *Name the first elected female governor in the United States.*

8.   *List some important physical landmarks in the region.*

If you have a limited time to review the chapter, you should start by reading these objectives and listing your familiarity with each topic, as in the sample below.

SAMPLE OBJECTIVE ASSESSMENT

1.   I can name most of these — Connecticut, Delaware, Maine, Massachusetts, New Hampshire, New York, Pennsylvania, and Vermont. I know I am missing a couple, so I had better look those up.

2.   I am not familiar with this topic at all.

3.   We watched a movie about agriculture in the Northeast in class and I feel comfortable with this topic.

4. I remember reading an article in class about Thomas Gilpin, who modernized papermaking in 1817 in Delaware.

5. I remember hearing about the Fundamental Orders, but I do not remember what they were.

6. The only one I know is Thomas Gilpin.

7. We read about Ella Grasso in class.

8. I am not familiar with this topic.

In this example, the student who completed the assessment could save time by focusing on the sections that cover objectives 1, 2, 5, 6, and 8, and skimming over the information that is already familiar. When time is available, the student would benefit from reading the entire chapter carefully. The most efficient use of limited time would be to concentrate on the unfamiliar concepts.

When looking over familiar material, try to locate definitions and concepts you do not know. You may discover that you need to read the sections more carefully, or you may find that in just a few minutes, you have filled in any information gaps.

Tip 30: Read for content using the SQ3R method.

The SQ3R method for critical reading consists of five basic steps: survey, question, read, recite, and review. The SQ3R method is especially useful for reading textbooks, but it can also be used to read short stories, magazine articles, and even novels.

The first step of SQ3R is to survey the assigned reading material. Read the titles, headings, introduction, conclusion, and summary. Look at any diagrams, pictures, and maps. Read captions and highlighted boxes. If your teacher gave you an assignment related to the subject, read it and note any ideas or questions you have.

The second step of SQ3R, reading, can be completed while you survey the reading. As you read the headings and subheadings of each section, try to turn the statements into questions. Write these questions down. For example, a chapter in a history textbook may have the heading "Causes of the Civil War." You could turn this heading into the question "What were some causes of the Civil War?" or "What caused the Civil War?"

Unless the section under the heading is only two or three sentences long, try to avoid questions that can be answered with a single date, word, or name. Approach the SQ3R method as a way to learn the material and prepare for future tests and assignments, not as a series of steps to rush through as quickly as possible. The following chart gives some examples of possible section headings from high school textbooks. The second column shows ineffective questions based on the headings. These questions would be quick and easy to answer, but would most likely not help the student develop a full understanding of the concepts covered in the section. The third column includes better questions based on the section headings.

Survey and Question Using SQ3R		
Section Heading	Ineffective Question	Better Question
The Start of World War II	When did World War II start?	What events signaled the start of World War II?
The Discovery of the Neutron	Who discovered the neutron?	How was the neutron discovered?

Survey and Question Using SQ3R		
How Alcohol Affects the Body	What is one way alcohol affects the body?	What are some affects of alcohol on the body?
Applying the Quadratic Formula	What is the quadratic formula?	How do you use the quadratic formula?

Effective questions address the complete section instead of focusing on one small detail. This helps you see how the pieces of information fit together.

Use the questions you wrote while surveying the chapter to guide you as you complete step three of the SQ3R method — read. As you read, look for the answers to the questions you framed from the headings and subheadings. Write the answers down as you find them. Pay close attention to captions and definitions. If you do not understand a section, read it again slowly.

After you read each section, take a few minutes to use your own words to explain the concepts before moving to the next section. If possible, recite key ideas aloud. Recite is the second R in SQ3R. Write your explanations down in your notes.

The last step of SQ3R is to review what you read. Look over the assigned reading and the notes you took. Reread anything you do not understand or remember. Use the questions you formed from the headings and subheadings to quiz yourself. Recite lists, dates, and definitions that you think are important.

You should not try to complete the SQ3R process in a single study session. Plan ahead and start early so that you have plenty of time to review the reading before a test. The more often you read and recite your notes, the more information you will retain.

The following example goes through the steps of the SQ3R process on a short sample passage.

USING THE SQ3R PROCESS

Sample Passage: The Role of Gender in German Grammar

German nouns are divided into three categories: masculine, feminine, and neuter. The gender of a noun does not depend on the qualities of the object the word describes, but on how the word is treated grammatically. In particular, the gender of a noun determines how the plural is formed, the corresponding pronoun, and the correct articles.

Identifying Masculine Nouns

The group of masculine nouns includes most words that refer to males, the days of the week, the months, and words that end in "-er," "-el," or "-en." Foreign words that are pronounced with an accent on the last syllable are also masculine.

Identifying Feminine Nouns

Feminine nouns include some words that refer to females, the names of numbers, names of rivers, and words that end in "-e." In addition, words that end in "-ei," "-schaft," "-heit," "-nz," "-keit," "-ie," "-k," and "-ion" are feminine.

Identifying Neuter Nouns

Diminutives that end in "-chen" or "-lein" are neuter nouns. Infinitives that act as nouns and nouns that begin with "Ge-" are also in this category, as are nouns that end in "-nis," -ment," "-um," "-tel," or "-tum."

Step	Implementation
Survey	Read the subtitles in the passage.
Question	Write questions based on the subtitles: • What role does gender play in German grammar? • How do you identify masculine nouns? • How do you identify feminine nouns? • How to you identify neuter nouns?

Step	Implementation
Read	Read the passage. Look for answers to the questions formed in the previous step. Write the answers down.
	What role does gender play in German grammar? Gender determines how the plural is formed, the corresponding pronoun, and the correct articles.
	How do you identify masculine nouns? Masculine nouns refer to males, the days of the week, the months, foreign words that are pronounced with an accent on the last syllable, and words that end in "-er," "-el," or "-en."
	How do you identify feminine nouns? Feminine nouns include some words that refer to females, the names of numbers, names of rivers, and words that end in "-e," "-ei," "-schaft," "-heit," "-nz," "-keit," "-ie," "-k," and "-ion."
	How do you identify neuter nouns? Neuter nouns begin with "Ge-," end with "-chen," -lein," "-nis," -ment," "-um," "-tel," or "-tum." Infinitives that act as nouns are neuter.
Recite	Repeat the answers identified in the previous step. Try to say them with your eyes closed.
Review	Reread sections that you do not understand. Look over answers that you have trouble remembering.

The SQ3R method can guide your reading of textbooks and increase your understanding of the material, but it is not a magic charm for learning. Like any technique, its effectiveness depends on how much effort you put in.

Tip 31: Create outlines to help you read for content.

Outlines are a way to see the structure of a story, essay, chapter, or book. Creating an outline of an assigned reading has many possible benefits. For example:

🕮 Outlines can help you see the connections between concepts or events.

☙   In creating an outline, you need to read carefully enough to identify main and supporting ideas.

☙   A completed outline can be a helpful studying tool. When reviewing material, you can read your outline instead of skimming the chapter.

☙   A good outline can be used as a guide when making flashcards, flap books, and slide cards.

☙   An outline can be completed in stages, letting you spread the reading process over several study sessions.

In a formal outline, the main ideas are listed using Roman numerals. Topics that support each main idea are listed using capital letters. Details that support these topics are numbered. If another layer of information is needed, the details are listed using lowercase letters. The structure of a formal outline is summarized in the chart below.

Formal Outline Structure
I.) FIRST MAIN IDEA
A.) Topic that supports first main idea
1) Supporting detail
(a) Additional information
(b) Additional information
2.) Supporting detail
(a) Additional information
(b) Additional information
B.) Topic that supports first main idea
1.) Supporting detail
(a)Additional information
(b)Additional information
2.) Supporting detail
(a) Additional information
(b) Additional information

Formal Outline Structure

II.) SECOND MAIN IDEA
  A.)   Topic that supports second main idea
    1.) Supporting detail
      (a) Additional information
      (b) Additional information
    2.) Supporting detail
      (a) Additional information
      (b) Additional information
  B.) Topic that supports second main idea
    1.) Supporting detail
      (a) Additional information
      (b) Additional information
    2.) Supporting detail
      (a) Additional information
      (b) Additional information

When writing an outline, not all main ideas will necessarily have the same number or depth of supporting information.

When reading a textbook, use headings and subheadings to form the initial structure of the outline. As you read the chapter, fill in the supporting details. If you are writing an outline by hand, it is difficult to know how much room you will need to leave for details under each topic. If you use a computer, this is not a concern. Some word processing programs have built-in tools that automate outline numbering.

The following example shows how a textbook selection could be outlined.

Sample Passage

Photography and Global Climate Change.

One way scientists track global change is through historical photographs. Researchers can study the size and position of glaciers in older photographs and compare the data to the glaciers' current position. From this information, they can calculate how global temperatures have changed over the last century.

Sample Passage

Concerns about Glacial Photographs

Many photographs taken in the 19th and early 20th centuries are stored on their original glass photographic slides in museum and private collections. Glass slides are brittle and may break easily. If not stored properly, they may be damaged by mold, sunlight, water, or air.

In addition to the threat of physical damage, some glacial photographs remain unavailable to the international scientific community because curators do not understand their significance. Other photographs are inaccessible because of political issues.

Southern Glacial Records

Currently, most of the glacial photographs available to climate researchers are of Northern glaciers. Only about 30 percent show glaciers in the Southern hemisphere. Without more information about historical weather patterns in the South, scientists are unable to form a complete picture of global climate change.

The Importance of Studying Past Climate Change

Scientists use information they gather about past weather behavior to help predict how the climate will change in the future. This is important because there are few human endeavors that are not influenced by the environment. If researchers can form better models to predict the weather, farmers will be able to make more informed decisions about what crops to plant, medical workers will be able to prepare for the most likely epidemics, and engineers will have more information about what natural disasters they should prepare structures against.

Passage Outline

I.) Photography and Global Climate Change
    A.) Concerns about Glacial Photographs
        1.) 19th and 20th century photographs may be stored on glass slides
            (a) Brittle, easy to break
            (b) May be damaged by mold, sunlight, water, or air
        2.) Photographs may be unavailable to international scientific community
            (a) Curators do not understand importance
            (b) Political issues
    B.) Southern Glacial Records
        1.) Most available glacial photographs are from Northern hemisphere
        2.) About 30 percent are of Southern glaciers

Passage Outline

3.) Southern glacial photographs needed to form a more complete picture of global climate change
II.) The Importance of Studying Past Climate Change
   A) Information about past weather helps scientists predict future weather
   B) Applications
      1.) Agriculture: farmers know what crops to plant
      2.) Medical: workers can plan for epidemics
      3.) Engineering: engineers know what natural disasters are likely

When reading material without headings and subheadings, creating an outline can be more challenging. One strategy for developing a structure for these passages is to find and list the main idea of each paragraph. Use this list as the highest level of organization in an outline. Complete the outline by filling in supporting details from the material.

In example below, the ideas listed with Roman numerals (I, II, III, and IV) correspond to the main topics of the essay's paragraphs. Because they are so closely related, the last two paragraphs are combined into one section of the outline.

Sample Passage Without Headings
Jane Austen
The author of some of the most enduring and famous romantic comedies of the period, Jane Austen, was born on December 16, 1775, in Hampshire, England. She was the seventh child in a family of six sons and two daughters. Although she wrote extensively about the manners and whims of the gentry, her father was a clergyman. Even though her family was not wealthy, they lived comfortably and had the resources to educate the children and help them pursue their interests.
Jane and her sister, Cassandra, attended school briefly, but they received most of their education at home where they studied modern languages, music, and history.
Like many of the heroines in her novels, Jane had a close relationship with her older sister. Cassandra was her confidant and constant companion. Even after her father died when she was 30, Jane continued to live with her mother and sister.

Sample Passage Without Headings

They survived with financial help from Jane's brothers and other family members. Although her writing is known for showing an insight into romantic love, Jane never married. She died when she was only 42 years old.

Although her career was cut short, Jane Austen wrote several novels about life and relationships in Regency England. Some of her most famous books include *Sense and Sensibility*, *Pride and Prejudice*, *Mansfield Park*, and *Emma*.

Sense and Sensibility, published in 1811, chronicles the tumultuous experiences of three sisters as they search for husbands and security after the death of their father leaves them destitute. Pride and Prejudice, published in 1813, focuses on a family of five young women, whose mother is intent on finding them rich husbands. In Mansfield Park, published a year later, Fanny Price is a poor girl struggles to fit into society after she is raised by her wealthy aunt and uncle. Fanny is quite a different character than the title character of Emma, published in 1816. Emma Woodhouse is a wealthy, confident, and poised heiress who causes misunderstandings when she plays matchmaker in her small town.

Passage Outline

I.) Birth and Early Years
    A.) Born on December 16, 1775 in Hampshire, England
    B.) The seventh of eight children
        1.) Six brothers
        2.) One sister
    C.) Father was a clergyman
    D.) Family was not wealthy, but able to live comfortably
II.) Education
    A.) Attended school briefly, mainly educated at home
    B.) Studied modern languages, music, and history
III.) Personal Life
    A.) Very close to her older sister, Cassandra
    B.) Lived with her sister and mother after her father died when she was 30
    C.) Never married
    D.) Died at age 42
IV.) Notable Works
    A.) *Sense and Sensibility*
        1.) Published in 1811
        2.) Plot summary: Three sisters search for husbands after the death of their
            father leaves them destitute.

Passage Outline
B.) *Pride and Prejudice*
1.) Published in 1813
2.) Plot summary: A mother searches for husbands for her five daughters.
C.) *Mansfield Park*
1.) Published in 1814
2.) Plot summary: A poor girl is raised by her rich relatives.
D.) *Emma*
1.) Published in 1816
2.) Plot summary: Wealthy Emma Woodhouse plays matchmaker in her small town.

An outline distills written material into the most important facts. Because it is more concise than the original reading, an outline is portable and faster to review.

When constructing an outline, pay attention to definitions, dates, and lists. Try to determine how the information fits together and use the relationships you identify to help you decide where to place facts within your outline.

The benefits of creating an outline are not limited to nonfiction material. You can also use outlines to summarize novels, short stories, and plays. An outline can help you:

- Read the material critically

- Participate in class discussions

- Develop topics for compositions

- Study for exams

- Identify repeated elements in the work

☙   Understand character motivation and development

☙   Recall plot details

☙   Recognize points to ask your teacher about

There are several ways to organize an outline of a short story or novel. You can use chapters, scenes, main characters, topics, or time to create the highest level of the outline's structure. Depending on the piece you are reading, you may want to include plotlines, character developments, setting notes, or dialogue excerpts in the lower divisions of the outline. When reading a piece of fiction critically, you may find creating several outlines using different structures increases your insight and understanding.

Compare the two following outlines of the same story. Together they summarize the main points of the material and give a more complete picture of the plot and character development than the individual outlines.

Character-based Outline

I.) Pauline
   A.) Relationships with other characters
      1.) Sarah's younger sister
      2.) Ford's classmate
      3.) Daughter of Claire and Doug
   B.) Background
      1.) Always lived in Sarah's shadow
      2.) Moved to a small Midwestern town with her family
   C.) Characteristics at beginning of novel
      1.) Always feels inferior to Sarah
      2.) Keeps to herself at school
      3.) Lonely and shy
   D.) Key events relating to
      1.) Assigned to work with Ford on a class art project
      2.) Discovers talent for and interest in sculpting
      3.) Applies to art school

Character-based Outline

    E.) Changes by end of novel
        1.) Develops more self-confidence
        2.) Finds identity outside "Sarah's younger sister"
        3.) Begins friendship with Ford and other classmates

II.) Sarah
    A.) Relationships with other characters
        1.) Pauline's older sister
        2.) Daughter of Claire and Doug
        3.) Dates Ford
    B.) Background
        1.) Popular and beautiful basketball star in their old town
        2.) Adapted to new town quickly
    C.) Characteristics at beginning of novel
        1.) Confident
        2.) Little empathy toward sister
    D.) Key events relating to
        1.) Breaks leg in key moment of championship game
        2.) Becomes depressed and withdrawn after injury
        3.) Models for Pauline and Ford's sculpture
    E.) Changes by end of novel
        1.) Possesses more empathy toward and understanding of Pauline
        2.) Develops identity beyond basketball star

III.) Ford
    A.) Relationships with other characters
        1.) Sarah's classmate
        2.) Pauline's classmate
        3.) Dates Sarah for a short time
    B.) Background
        1.) Lives with his grandparents
        2.) Parents died in a car accident when he was an infant
    C.) Characteristics at beginning of novel
        1.) Quiet, smart student who always makes good grades
        2.) No social life, stays at home so he will not worry his grandparents
    D.) Key events relating to
        1.) Assigned to work with Pauline on a class art project
        2.) Meets and develops a romantic relationship with Sarah
    E.) Changes by end of novel
        1.) Has a life outside school
        2.) Builds foundation for independence from grandparents

Chapter-based Outline

I.) Chapter 1
  A.) Structure
    1.) Written from Pauline's point of view
    2.) Covers events from Pauline and Sarah learning about the move through the first half of the championship game
  B.) Main events
    1.) Pauline, Sarah, and their parents move to a small Midwestern town
    2.) Sarah immediately fits in at the new high school and on the basketball team
    3.) Pauline eats by herself, has trouble meeting people at school
  C.) Key quotes
    1.) "The kids at Harrison Smith High School were just like the people everywhere we had ever been. They loved Sarah immediately." -Pauline
    2.) "She's nobody important, just my sister." -Sarah
    3.) "My parents have one expression on their face when they look at Sarah, and a completely different one when they look at me." -Pauline
  D.) Important imagery and symbolism
    1.) Pauline's fascination with Antarctica, a place as unwelcoming as she is
    2.) Pauline sees her classmates as a group, never refers to anyone individually except Sarah; they are all anonymous and identical to her

II.) Chapter 2
  A.) Structure
    1.) Written from Ford's point of view
    2.) Covers events from Pauline and Sarah's arrival at the school through the beginning stages of work on Ford and Pauline's art project
  B.) Main events
    1.) Ford sees Sarah and forms an instant crush
    2.) Sarah breaks her leg in the championship basketball game
    3.) Ford is assigned Pauline as his partner on a class art project
  C.) Key quotes
    1.) "I vaguely remembered her from class. I think she sat in the middle somewhere. Then I saw her last name and I wondered if she was related to Sarah." -Ford
    2.) "Sarah crumbled like a tower of children's blocks. The crowd was silent by the time she hit the ground." -Ford
  D.) Important imagery and symbolism
    1.) Sarah as a band director, leading the crowd's gasps and cheers as she plays basketball
    2.) Ford's parents as the gods of his family tribe — never seen, but always present and needing to be pleased

Chapter-based Outline

III.) Chapter 3
  A.) Structure
    1.) Written from Sarah's point of view
    2.) Covers events from Sarah's injury through completion of Ford and Pauline's art project
  B.) Main events
    1.) Sarah stops going to class and after school activities, feels forgotten by former friends
    2.) Ford and Pauline ask Sarah to model for their art project
    3). Ford and Sarah kiss
  C.) Key quotes
    1.) "There's a comfort in being invisible, a strange happiness in being forgotten." -Sarah
    2.) "You just have to sit there looking maudlin for a few hours. It's not like you have to change your daily routine." -Pauline
  D.) Important imagery and symbolism
    1.) Sarah's comparison as her cast as a cocoon
    2.) Sarah's obsession with the dying plant in the foyer
IV.) Chapter 4
  A.) Structure
    1.) Written from Pauline's point of view
    2.) Covers events from Pauline's application to art school through the end of the school year
  B.) Main events
    1.) Sarah returns to school, but refuses to be swept up in social cliques
    2.) Pauline realizes she is a talented artist
    3.) Pauline works up the courage to talk to the girl she shares a work bench with in art class
  4.) Pauline applies to art school
  C.) Key quotes
    1.) "I expected to be relieved when the sculpture was finished, but I was sad. It seemed like the time had passed too quickly." -Pauline
    2.) "'Your painting is beautiful,' I told her. 'I love how you used watercolors over the acrylics.' She looked up at me and for a second I thought there would be that expression of surprise and disdain that people always get when I talk. Instead, she smiled." -Pauline
  D.) Important imagery and symbolism
    1.) Pauline starts to refer to classmates by individual characteristics
    2.) Pauline's perception that the windows of her home and school seemed to be larger as a symbol that she was letting people see more of her

Do not use purchased, copied, or borrowed outlines as substitutes for reading assigned material. You are likely to learn more from creating your own outline than from simply studying one prepared by another student. If you rely on another person's summary of the important concepts contained in an assigned reading, you may be saving time, but you will be depriving yourself of the opportunity to develop the strongest possible understanding of the material.

Tip 32: Compare your notes to the summary and vocabulary list at the end of the chapter.

If your textbook includes chapter summaries, use this feature to help you assess how well you understand the material you have read. When reviewing a chapter summary, keep the following questions in mind:

- How well do understand each concept in the summary?

- Do you see how the concepts in the chapter are related?

- Does the summary touch on any subjects that you did not think were important when you read the chapter?

- Are you able to remember information that the summary left out?

Have a sheet of paper in front of you and a pencil in your hand while you read a summary. Take notes on any information that seems unfamiliar so that you can reread the appropriate sections in the chapter. Quiz yourself by asking questions about the causes of, effects from, and connections between the concepts in the summary.

In addition to summaries, some textbooks may include a list of important terms used in each chapter. Students can use these vocabulary lists can be used in a variety of ways, including:

- Challenge yourself to provide the definition for each term without looking in the glossary or text.

- Make flashcards or a flap book of the terms and definitions.

- List the vocabulary words on a sheet of paper, leaving several lines between each word. Reread the chapter. As you come to a term on the vocabulary list, try to write a definition in your own words based on the information in the chapter.

Vocabulary lists and chapter summaries can help you review and evaluate your understanding of textbook material. They can help you determine what the textbook's author thought were the most important concepts and what you may need to pay more attention to. Summaries are not substitutes for reading the chapter. Because summaries reduce 20 to 30 pages of information into a few short paragraphs, if you only read the shortened version then you are likely to miss important details and fail to form a good understanding of the material.

Tip 33: Practice reading.

Reading assigned material helps you learn new concepts and reinforces ideas introduced in class or laboratory experiences. When completing a reading assignment, your goals may include:

- Understanding what you read

- Reading efficiently so you have time to work on other tasks

- Remembering information in the material

- Identifying connections between key concepts

Reading is a skill, just like managing time, shooting hook shots, or performing a pirouette. No matter how good you are at reading, there is always room for improvement. The only way to develop your reading skills is to practice. You do not have to read textbooks and encyclopedias in your spare time. By reading for pleasure, you can learn to read faster by picking out important details without having to read every word and become better at understanding the tone and implications of written material. In addition, reading can be a relaxing and inexpensive activity.

The wider variety of material you read, the more opportunities you have to develop your reading proficiency. For fun, you may enjoy reading:

- Magazines   - Novels

- Nonfiction books   - Web sites

- Newspapers   - Game manuals

- Plays

If you have trouble finding reading material that interests you, visit your local library or bookstore to find books and periodicals about your favorite hobby, sport, or celebrity.

Reading for pleasure should not be a chore. You do not need to set a plan or chart your improvement. If you find that you love a particular book, give yourself permission to reread it as much as you want. If you find a play boring, find one that is more intriguing. When you read for fun, you do not need to memorize details, analyze characters, or think about symbolism. You may find that those tasks come more naturally as you become a more skillful reader.

Case Study: Coby L. Ringgenberg

Coby L. Ringgenberg

College Residence Life Supervisor

When reading a chapter, I take notes and outline the key points, which are the headings, the bolded print, and the first sentence of each paragraph. That helps me understand what I am reading and retain the information.

Taming Long-Term Assignments

Schoolwork can be divided into two broad categories: short-term and long-term. Short-term work includes homework that is due, reading of material that will be covered, and studying for tests that will be administered within a week of being announced. Long-term assignments occur on a longer time scale than a week. They require more work than short-term assignments.

Benefits of Long-term Assignments

Long-term assignments can be challenging, but they can also help you develop new skills. If you have trouble remaining focused and motivated while working on a project that spans several study sessions, take into account that the assignment can help you become a better student by giving you an opportunity to:

Practice time management skills. If you need to complete a large project in addition to your regular homework load, you may need to find time for extra or longer study sessions.

See the big picture. An extended assignment can help illustrate the connections between concepts covered throughout the school year or topics covered in different courses.

Enhance understanding. A project can give you the opportunity to explore a topic in greater depth than the teacher can cover in class.

Explore a personal interest. You may be able to choose a topic or direction for the assignment that intrigues you but that would not be covered in class.

Prepare for higher education. Long-term assignments become increasingly common through college and graduate school. If you plan to continue your education after high school, consider the project as practice for your future academic career.

Explore your creativity. Large projects offer more flexibility in planning and implementation than typical geometry problems and Spanish conjugations. As much as you can while still fulfilling the requirements of the assignment, use your talents and skills to personalize the project and keep it fun. If you are interested in film production, add a multimedia aspect to your class presentation. If you enjoy creating art, add a personal touch to your science fair project display.

Develop problem solving skills. The more complicated and time consuming a project, the greater the chance that something will not go exactly according to plan. Your computer might crash, one step of the assignment might take longer to finish than you expected, or you might run out of an important supply. As frustrating as these snags can be, they can also be opportunities to learn about alternative ways of completing tasks and staying calm under tight deadlines.

Increase confidence. Take pride in successfully planning and completing a long-term project. Use it as proof of your abilities and perseverance.

Learn to work independently and as part of a team. If you mostly work as part of a group in class, completing an individual project can help you identify new talents. If you complete most of your assignments alone, a group project can help you develop teamwork and cooperation skills.

Types of Long-term Projects

Throughout high school, you may encounter several types of large assignments, each with different requirements and benefits.

Papers

Papers are assignments that are primarily written. Although your final draft may include diagrams or illustrations, the focus of a paper is on the words. You may be assigned papers in nearly any class, including English, music, history, science, and even physical education. No matter what subject your paper is for, it is important to use correct spelling and grammar.

Unless your teacher specifically asks you to write the paper by hand, use a computer or typewriter so that your work is neat. If your teacher gives you an outline or template to use when writing the paper, follow it exactly. Otherwise, format your paper simply and professionally. Some common formatting choices include:

- Title centered in the middle of the first page

- One or one and a half inch margins on all four sides

- A font that is simple and easy-to-read

- Black ink

- Left justification

- Five space indention at the beginning of a paragraph

The mechanics of your paper should showcase, not distract from, your writing. Unless your teacher specifically tells you differently, avoid fancy fonts, overly small or large type, and colored paper.

Proofread your paper carefully before you turn it in. Look for and correct any spelling or grammatical errors. Some of the most common writing problems include:

Subject and verb do not agree

Incorrect: School, cheer practice, and work is wearing me out.
Correct: School, cheer practice, and work are wearing me out.

Two possible meanings

Incorrect: She still learns calligraphy from her home.
Correct: She still learns calligraphy at her home.

Incorrect pronoun

Incorrect: Mary, John, him, and me are on the committee.
Correct: Mary, John, he, and I are on the committee.

Nonparallel structure

Incorrect: Various sites throughout the world have been a source
of inspiration.

Correct: Various sites throughout the world have been sources of inspiration.

CONFUSING ADJECTIVES WITH ADVERBS

Incorrect: Throw the ball soft.
Correct: Throw the ball softly.

DANGLING MODIFIERS

Incorrect: The helicopter touched the ground, with a roar from the crowd.
Correct: As it touched the ground, the helicopter was greeted with a roar from the crowd.

If you have trouble identifying writing errors, consider asking a parent, friend, or teacher to review your work.

Research Papers

A research paper is more than just a long essay. Whether you come up with your own topic or are assigned one, to complete a research paper you will need to find appropriate sources, use those sources to develop your topic, and site your sources correctly.

Creative Writing

Creative writing assignments include short stories, poems, and plays. When completing a creative writing assignment, it is important to know what your teacher is looking for in the final draft. If you are required to copy a historic style such as a sonnet or Greek drama, take into account that your teacher will be grading your project on how well it demonstrates your understanding of that style. If the assignment is in a foreign language course, your teacher is likely to be looking for how well you use the vocabulary and grammar rules learned in class. In literature classes, you may be expected to use a specific technique or write within a particular genre.

Literature Reviews

A literature review summarizes books and articles about a particular topic. The depth to which you will have to discuss each source will depend on the class, topic, and assignment requirements. When writing a research paper, you use information from several different sources to draw conclusions about your topic. In a literature review, you discuss each book or article separately. You may be expected to give your opinions about the strengths and weaknesses of each source. Your teacher may give you a list of sources to use for your literature review, or you may be expected to find appropriate material yourself.

Laboratory Reports

A laboratory report is a written discussion of the purpose of, procedure used, and results from an experiment or other hands-on activity. In a laboratory report, you may be required to state your hypothesis and the conclusions you were able to draw from the results. Laboratory reports are written in the third person. It is acceptable to use the passive voice, especially when discussing how the experiment was conducted. For example, you may prefer to write "three milligrams of NaCl were added to the solution" instead of "we added three milligrams of NaCl to the solution." Your teacher may require you to include an abstract of your report. An abstract is a short summary of the important points of your report. When grading a laboratory report, your teacher will be looking for evidence that you understood why you performed the experiment, how the process worked, and what the results mean.

PRESENTATIONS

A presentation is a project whose end result will be shown to an audience. You may be required to write a paper to accompany your project or the presentation may be the entire assignment. Presentations can be divided into two categories: oral presentations and viewed presentations.

Oral Presentations

An oral presentation is any speech, debate, or demonstration that you compose and then deliver to your audience. When giving an oral presentation, you might use slides, posters, models, or computer images to help deliver your message and keep your audience's attention. Depending on the course for which you are preparing the presentation, you may be graded on your delivery, the content of your presentation, or both.

Viewed Presentations

Viewed presentations are those that the audience looks at without direct interaction with the presenter. Posters, displays, and multimedia productions are examples of viewed presentations. Even though you do not guide viewers through your presentation, you may be expected to be available to answer questions about your work.

EXPERIENTIAL PROJECTS

Experiential projects require intensive hands-on involvement.

Although you may need to consult reference materials to complete an experiential project, there is more emphasis on your original work. When grading experiential projects, teachers are likely to be as concerned about the method and techniques used as they are with the results.

Science Projects

To complete a science project, you will need to work through the steps of the scientific process. This process includes researching a topic, identifying a problem or question, forming a hypothesis that predicts your answer to the question, developing and performing experiments to test your hypothesis, analyzing the results from your experiments, and drawing conclusions about how the results relate to your hypothesis. As part of a science project assignment, you may be required to share your results through an oral or viewed presentation.

Art Projects

An art project is a large scale creative assignment that requires you to research, develop, and implement a way to interpret an idea to a visual media. You may need to sketch your ideas, make models, and experiment with different materials to complete an art project. Your teacher may decide to grade your art project on technique, creativity, or both.

Group Projects

Group projects are collaborative efforts between two or more classmates. When you work with other people, you will not get to make all the decisions. One of the challenges of group projects is learning how to merge several people's ideas. Successful teams are those whose members know when to compromise about an issue and when to stand their ground. While working on a group project, you may find yourself in an uncomfortable role. If you are quick to make decision, you may find it difficult to work with your teammate to reach a consensus about major project concerns. If you are a quiet person, you may feel uneasy speaking up if you feel a teammate is making a mistake.

Other Projects

Experiential assignments can give students a taste of how professionals conceive and develop projects. They are a way for students and teachers to learn about topics that are too specific or contemporary to be covered in class. Experiential projects can be a fun and effective learning tool in almost any subject.

Music theory: Advanced music students may be assigned large musical compositions to demonstrate a concept or showcase the strengths of an instrument.

Computer science: Computer science students may need to write a program to solve a hypothetical or real-life problem.

Foreign languages: Experiential projects for foreign language classes include large translation or interpretation assignments.

Physical education: Participating in, planning, training for, and refereeing a sporting event are examples of experiential physical education projects.

Math: Mathematics students may be assigned complicated proofs or problems that require research and several days of work to solve.

PERFORMANCES

Performances are closely related to oral presentations in that the student is expected to present the prepared work to the audience. While oral presentations are composed by the student, performances are created by an author, composer, or choreographer. In addition to accuracy, your teacher may expect your performance to show a degree of artistry.

Performances are often assigned in music or drama classes. You may need to prepare a dramatic reading for a language arts, foreign language, speech, or history class, or participate in a skit for health or psychology. Auditions are specialized projects where a judge grades your performance.

Whether you are appearing in a school play, presenting a dramatic reading to your American history class, or auditioning for a music scholarship, the basic steps for completing the performance project are the same.

Research the requirements. The first step in preparing for a performance is to research the requirements. If you are auditioning for a group, school, or scholarship, make sure you have the official requirements in writing. Do not rely on your memory or on secondhand information. If you are preparing for a class assignment, be sure that you understand the grading criteria. Clarify if you need to prepare supplemental material such as a report or bibliography. Find out if you need any special clothing or props.

Gather your materials. Once you know the performance requirements, gather the scores or scripts you need. If you get to choose your own material, try to find pieces that you enjoy playing. When preparing for an audition, look for material that showcases your strengths and downplays your weaknesses. If you have trouble deciding between two or more pieces, consider asking for your teacher's opinion.

Collect references. Look for pictures, recordings, or live performances of the material you are preparing. Listen to or watch your source material critically. Take notes about what you enjoyed about the performances and what you would do differently. Do not copy anyone else's performance. Instead, use their interpretation and execution of the material as an inspiration for your own.

Create a preparation schedule. List everything you need to do before the performance. This might include learning the pieces, putting together an outfit, and gathering props. Divide the items on this list into tasks and create a schedule that will allow you to finish them all before your performance.

Practice for accuracy. Work through the technical parts of the piece first. Pay extra attention to challenging passages.

Practice for artistry. Once you can play, sing, or recite your piece well, think about how different inflections and volumes could improve your performance. Review your references and note other performers' phrasing.

Solicit feedback. As you master sections of the piece, play for teachers, parents, classmates, or friends and ask for their responses. Use their feedback to help polish your performance. Try not to take any criticism personally. Do not become defensive about your performance or get mad at your listener. Blind accolades will not help you improve.

Schedule a dry run. Once you can perform your pieces accurately and artistically, arrange for a dress rehearsal. Make this dry run as similar to the actual performance as possible. Wear the clothes and use the props you have prepared. If possible, hold this dry run where you will perform. A dress rehearsal can help you identify possible problems or holes in your preparation. For example, you might find that your costume is overly restricting or that your shoes slide dangerously across the stage. Try not to be frustrated at any issues your dress rehearsal reveals. Instead, be glad you learned about the problems in time to correct them before the actual performance. If your schedule permits, consider arranging for more than one dress rehearsal so that you can identify and correct as many problems as possible.

Relax. It is common to be nervous about a performance, but tension can cause you to perform below your potential. Your favorite downtime activity might help you relax. Exercising, meditating, soaking in a hot tub, or reading a novel may help relieve some performance anxiety.

Keep your perspective. Trust in the preparation you have invested in your performance. Try not to dwell on mistakes or regret not practicing more.

Review your performance. After your performance, think about what you did well and in what areas you could have done better. Ask yourself if your performance would have benefited by any changes in your preparation schedule. Write down any suggestions you have for future performances.

Whether you are working on a paper, presentation, experiential project, or performance, the tips in this chapter can help you finish the assignment on time, completely, and in a way that demonstrates your mastery of the material.

Case Study: Marilyn K. Wilson

Marilyn K. Wilson

High School Teacher

When practicing different rhythm patterns for music class, I have students walk or skip the note values. It looks a little silly, but it is effective.

Tip 34: Start working on the project as soon as possible.

If you rush a long assignment, you are depriving yourself of the opportunity to turn in your best possible work. By beginning work on your project early, you will be giving yourself several advantages.

More opportunities to add creative touches to the project: If you give yourself enough time to work on the assignment at a relaxed pace, you might see new ways to approach the project and more chances to infuse it with your personal style. If you only have a short time to throw the project together, you are limiting yourself to the obvious and easy choices.

More time to clarify the assignment: As you work on the project, you may find that you have questions about requirements, grading criteria, or schedule. If you have not waited until the last minute to get started, you have more time to consult with your teacher and make sure you understand the assignment.

More time to find and order reference material: If you order a book through an online source or request a periodical by interlibrary loan, weeks may pass before you have the material in your hands. If you wait until a week before a term paper is due to start working on it and finding material, it may be hard to find the resources you need.

More time to revise: The earlier you complete a draft of your project, the more time you will have to polish your work and add details. Some students justify procrastination by claiming that they work better on a tight deadline. Odds are that they do not work better; they have just lowered their standards.

More time to correct errors or deal with the unexpected: Colds, power outages, and family emergencies can derail the most conscientiously prepared schedule. The earlier you start on your project, the more time you will have to make up for unavoidably missed study sessions.

Less stress from a tight deadline: The less time you have to complete an assignment, the more you have to think about decisions, handle problems, and take some time away from the project to relax. The results of not starting a large assignment early are often more anxiety, lost sleep, and a low grade.

Less work to do at every study session: Every large assignment can be divided into a series of smaller tasks that need to be completed. The earlier you start working on your project, the more days you have to spread these tasks across.

Less chance of turning the project in late or incomplete: If you procrastinate long enough, you may find you have waited too long to start and there is no way to finish the project on time.

Despite the benefits of starting a long-term project early, some students still find reasons to put off beginning their large assignments. There are many excuses for not starting a project.

There is not enough time to work on the project. Delaying the start of a project is seldom a good idea. Busy schedules tend to stay busy and there may never be a perfect time to work on the project. On days that are packed with homework, personal obligations, and after school activities, even 10 or 15 minutes of focused work on the assignment can result in real progress and save future frustration.

There is plenty of time to get started. Do not procrastinate because the due date seems far in the future. If you underestimated how long the project will take to complete, you may leave yourself too little time to do the assignment well. The longer you wait to get started, the greater the risk that another assignment, a social event, or an illness will interfere with your work schedule.

The supplies are not available. If you have to order tools or books to complete your project, seek out tasks that you can complete while you wait for the resources to be delivered. Read and take notes on the materials you have available. Make sketches of possible presentation layouts. Create an outline to help organize your ideas.

Tip 35: Become a project manager.

In the corporate world, project managers divide large jobs into smaller tasks and create schedules to make sure the tasks are completed as efficiently as possible. You can use the same techniques that professional project managers employ to finish your long-term assignment as well as you can, with a minimum of wasted time.

As the project manager, one of your first jobs is to create a schedule. A project schedule is a timeline of estimated completion dates for intermediate stages of your project. As you work on your project, refer to the schedule to make sure you are progressing at a pace that will let you finish on time.

To create your timeline, you will need to list all the tasks that need to be done to finish the assignment. The following chart shows the list a student working on a term paper might make.

Term Paper Tasks

- Make a list of possible topics.

- Research available references for possible topics.

- Determine which topics have sufficient reference materials available.

- Decide between possible topics.

- Create a working bibliography.

- Order any necessary reference materials.

- Read and take notes on references.

- Organize notes on notecards.

- Determine a thesis for paper.

- List three to four supporting ideas.

- Review notes.

- Reorganize notecards based on relationship to supporting ideas.

- Compose outline based on thesis, supporting ideas, and notes.

- Fill in outline using complete sentences.

- Change outline into section headings and subheadings.

- Check draft for grammar and spelling errors.

- Rewrite unclear passages.

- Have study partner read and comment.

- Format manuscript.

- Add footnotes.

- Review your the bibliography and write the final bibliography.

- Reread final draft and make any corrections.

- Review formatting and correct any errors.

- Print manuscript, footnotes, and bibliography.

- Purchase report cover.

- Bind paper.

- Read through paper for the final time.

- Correct and reprint pages as needed.

Write each task on the center of an index card. Arrange the cards in chronological order so that the tasks you have to complete first are at the front of the pile and those that will not be finished until late in the process are at the end of the pile. For example, if you are writing a term paper, one of your early tasks would be to choose a topic. You will not need to purchase a report cover or print the final draft of the paper until closer to the assignment's due date.

Once you have the deck of task cards arranged, lay the cards out in order on the floor or a large table. Think about how the tasks are related and try to group them into major milestones toward the completion of the project. The following chart lists how the tasks from the example term paper project could be grouped by milestones.

Term Paper Milestones and Related Tasks	
Milestone	**Tasks**
Choose a Topic	Make a list of possible topics.
	Research available references for possible topics.
	Determine which topics have sufficient reference materials available.
	Decide between possible topics.
Research Topic	Create working bibliography.
	Order any necessary reference materials.
	Read and take notes on references.
	Organize notes on notecards.
Write Outline	Determine thesis for paper.
	List three to four supporting ideas.
	Review notes.
	Reorganize notecards based on relationship to supporting ideas.
	Compose outline based on thesis, supporting ideas and notes.
Write First Draft	Fill in outline using complete sentences.
	Change outline into section headings and subheadings.

Term Paper Milestones and Related Tasks	
Revise	Check draft for grammar and spelling errors.
	Rewrite unclear passages.
	Have study partner read and comment.
Write Final Draft	Format manuscript.
	Add footnotes.
	Review working bibliography and write final bibliography.
	Reread final draft and make any corrections.
Publish Paper	Review formatting and correct any errors.
	Print manuscript, footnotes, and bibliography.
	Purchase report cover.
	Bind paper.
	Read through final time.
	Correct and reprint pages as needed.

Write the name of the appropriate milestone at the top of each card. Keep your cards laid out in chronological order. Estimate how much time you think you will need to complete each task, and write this estimate in the lower right hand corner of the card as in the example below.

> Write final draft
>
> Review working bibliography and write final bibliography
>
> 120 minutes

Examine your cards and try to identify tasks that can be completed concurrently. For example, in the chart above the student may be able to create working bibliographies for each topic while investigating the availability of reference materials. Number each task based on the order they should be completed. Give tasks that can be worked on concurrently the same number followed by a unique letter. For example, if you plan to review and reorganize your notes at the same time, these might be labeled "4a" and "4b." Write the number of each task in the upper right hand corner of the appropriate card.

Now that the cards are in chronological order, estimate the total amount of time it will take to reach each milestone by adding the estimated completion times for the related tasks and adding 10 percent to the sum. This extra 10 percent will help protect your schedule and sanity if some tasks take longer to complete than you expect. Add the milestone completion times to estimate how long it will take to complete the entire project.

Completion Time Estimates		
Milestone	**Tasks**	**Estimated Completion Time (min)**
Choose a Topic	Make a list of possible topics.	60
	Research available references for possible topics.	360
	Determine which topics have sufficient reference materials.	20
	Decide between possible topics.	20
Total estimated minutes to choose a topic		**705**
Write Outline	Determine thesis for paper.	60
	List three to four supporting ideas.	45
	Review notes.	120
	Reorganize notecards based on relationship to supporting ideas.	60
	Compose outline based on thesis, supporting ideas, and notes.	120

Completion Time Estimates		
Total estimated minutes to write outline		405
Write first Draft	Fill in outline using complete sentences.	240
	Change outline into section headings and subheadings.	20
Total estimated minutes to write first draft		260
Revise	Check draft for grammar and spelling errors.	30
	Rewrite unclear passages.	60
	Have study partner read and comment.	30
Total estimated minutes to revise		120
Write final draft	Format manuscript.	20
	Add footnotes.	30
	Review working bibliography and write final bibliography.	120
	Reread final draft and make any corrections.	45
Total estimated minutes to write final draft		215
Publish Paper	Review formatting and correct any errors.	30
	Print manuscript, footnotes, and bibliography.	10
	Purchase report cove.r	20
	Bind paper.	10
	Read through final time.	20
	Correct and reprint pages as needed.	30
Total estimated minutes to publish paper		120
Total estimated minutes to write paper		2280 minutes = 38 hours

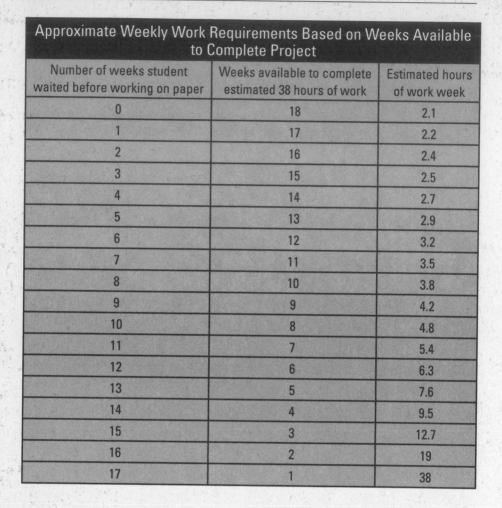

Approximate Weekly Work Requirements Based on Weeks Available to Complete Project		
Number of weeks student waited before working on paper	Weeks available to complete estimated 38 hours of work	Estimated hours of work week
0	18	2.1
1	17	2.2
2	16	2.4
3	15	2.5
4	14	2.7
5	13	2.9
6	12	3.2
7	11	3.5
8	10	3.8
9	9	4.2
10	8	4.8
11	7	5.4
12	6	6.3
13	5	7.6
14	4	9.5
15	3	12.7
16	2	19
17	1	38

If the student only waits a week or two to begin working on the term paper, there will not be a huge difference in the average amount of time required each week to complete the estimated 38 hours of work. If the student procrastinates until the middle of the semester, the workload balloons to more than four hours per week. If work is delayed until three weeks before the paper is due, finishing the assignment might feel like a part-time job.

Once you have calculated the estimated time needed to complete each task, the major milestones, and the complete project, review your calendar and count how many days you have to work on the project. Skip days that are already filled with personal, work, or school obligations. If you start your project early, you may need to work on the assignment only two or three days per week. On your calendar, use the project's name or an appropriate abbreviation to mark the days you plan to work on the assignment.

Divide the total time you estimate that it will take you to complete the project by the number of days you have to work on it in order to find out the average length of time you will have to devote toward the project per day. You may decide to work longer than the average on some days and shorter than the average on others, but this average calculation will help you create a working timeline for your project to help keep you on schedule.

Divide the estimated time to complete each task by the average amount of time needed per day to complete the project to approximate how many days it will take to finish each task. Use this information to calculate how many days you should allot for each major milestone.

The following table shows these calculations for the example term paper. These estimates assumed the student would need to spend an average of one hour per day working on the paper to complete it on time.

Project Schedule Calculations Summary			
Milestone	Tasks	Estimated Completion Time (min)	Approximate Number of Days to Complete at 1 Hour per Day
Choose a Topic			
	Make a list of possible topics.	60	1
	Research available references for possible topics.	360	6
	Determine which topics have sufficient reference materials available.	20	0.3

Project Schedule Calculations Summary

	Decide between possible topics.	20	0.3
	Total for milestone	460	7.6
Research a Topic			
	Create working bibliography.	60	1
	Order any necessary reference materials.	120	2
	Read and take notes on references.	480	8
	Organize notes on notecards.	45	0.75
	Total for milestone	705	11.75
Write Outline			
	Determine thesis for paper.	60	1
	List three to four supporting ideas.	45	0.75
	Review notes.	120	2
	Reorganize notecards based on relationship to supporting ideas.	60	1
	Compose outline based on thesis, supporting ideas and notes.	120	2
	Total for milestone	405	6.75
Write First Draft			
	Fill in outline using complete sentences.	240	4
	Change outline into section headings and subheadings.	20	0.3
	Total for milestone	260	4.3
Revise			
	Check draft for errors.	30	0.5
	Rewrite unclear passages.	60	1
	Have study partner read and comment.	30	0.5
	Total for milestone	120	2
Write Final Draft			
	Format manuscript.	20	0.3
	Add footnotes.	30	0.5
	Review working bibliography and write final bibliography.	120	2
	Reread final draft and make any corrections.	45	0.75
	Total for milestone	215	3.6
Publish Paper			
	Review formatting and correct errors.	30	0.5

Project Schedule Calculations Summary			
	Print manuscript, footnotes, and bibliography.	10	0.2
	Purchase report cover.	20	0.3
	Bind paper.	20	0.3
	Read through final time.	20	0.3
	Correct and reprint pages as needed.	30	0.5
	Total for milestone	120	2
	Approximate number of days to complete		38

After you have an estimate of the number of days it will take to complete each task, look back at your calendar. Using the days you have marked as project work days, assign tentative due dates to each task. The student working on the example term paper calculated that the first task, "make a list of possible topics," would take about one day to complete. The tentative due date for this task would be the end of the first scheduled work day. The next task, "research available reference for possible topics," should take about six days to finish. The due date for that task would be the seventh scheduled work day.

Some tasks may share a due date if they are small or will be worked on concurrently.

Write each task's tentative due date on the bottom left-hand corner of the task's card, as shown in the example below.

Write final draft 19a
Review working bibliography and write final bibliography
June 30 120 minutes

Keep the task cards in order. Keep them somewhere handy so you can review them when you work on the project. The card on top should correspond to the task you are currently working on. As you finish the task, write the actual completion date under the tentative due date and move the task card to the bottom of the pile.

Tentative deadlines can help you see how well you are adhering to the schedule you have set for your project, but they should not cause more stress in your life. For any project, some tasks will take less time than you expected and some will take longer. Do not use being ahead of schedule as an excuse to take a break from your project. Keep the extra time available in case a task requires more time than you have allotted. If you fall behind schedule, try not to panic. See if you can fit in additional work sessions or if you can shave some time off an upcoming task without sacrificing the quality of your work.

The following table summarizes the necessary steps to create a project schedule.

Creating a Project Schedule

1. List the tasks you need to do to complete the project.

2. Write each task on the center of an index card.

3. Arrange cards in the order you will complete the tasks.

4. Divide cards into major milestone categories based on how they are related. Write each task's major milestone category in the upper left hand corner of its card.

5. Estimate how long you think you will need to complete each task and write this number in the bottom right hand corner of the appropriate card.

6. Calculate the total amount of time need to complete the project by adding the estimated completion times for the tasks.

7. Schedule days to work on the project. Count how many days you have scheduled.

Creating a Project Schedule

8. Divide the total amount of time you estimate it will take to complete all the tasks by the number of days you have scheduled to work on the project. This will give you the average amount of time you will need to work on the project during each scheduled day.

9. Divide the estimate completion time on each card by the average work day length to determine how many days it will take to complete the task. Use this calculation to determine a tentative due date for each task. Write the tentative due date in the bottom left hand corner of the task card.

10. As you finish each task, write the actual date you finished under the tentative due date on the task card.

11. Pay attention to your tentative due dates as you work on the project. If you fall behind schedule, take steps to make up the lost time.

When you have finished your project, each task card will have the following information:

Major milestone category	Task number
Task Description	
Tentative Due Date	Approximate Completion Time
Date Finished	

Creating a project schedule may seem like substantial work, but it is an investment in time and labor. The more organized you are, the more smoothly your project will progress.

Case Study: Rick Boes

Rick Boes

Project Manager

At the start of a project, I review the material and labor estimates, break out a base schedule, and check the material availability and costs.

CLASSIFIED CASE STUDIES

directly from the experts

Case Study: Rick Boes

Basically, I build the project in my head and on paper. I think about possible problems, because when issues arise — and they will — I am able to recall the problem area and come to a speedy resolution. Time is money when a crew is waiting for an answer.

There is only so much time in a day, so make the best use of it. Use a day planner, either electronic or hand written. One thing that helps me, if I keep waking up in the middle of the night worrying about a job, is to keep a notepad on the nightstand. That way I can jot the thoughts down and go back to sleep instead of worrying the rest of the night about it.

Tip 36: Create a project file.

If you have to spend half of your scheduled work time looking for the right article, searching for a missing notebook, or rewriting a misplaced outline, you are more likely to fall behind schedule. A project file can help you work efficiently and avoid the frustration of lost paperwork and missing tools.

A project file includes the resources and tools you need to work on your long-term assignment. With an organized project file, you will be able to make progress even if you only have five minutes to devote to the assignment. Simply look at the top task card to see what needs to be done, grab the material you need, and get to work.

The contents of your project file depend on the assignment and where you are in your project schedule, but you may want to include some of the following:

Assignment requirements: If your teacher gives you a list of what you need to do for the project, make sure to keep a reference copy in your project file.

Project notebook: A notebook dedicated to the project can be useful to keep sketches, ideas, and reminders organized.

Receipts for ordered material: If you ordered materials from a dealer or through your library, keep the information handy so you know what resources are still outstanding. Try to find out who to talk to if the material does not arrive on time and keep their contact information with the receipts.

Books and articles you need to read: If you are using several large books as reference materials, you may want to keep only the ones you are currently using in your project file.

Current draft of project: Keep a copy of your project at its current level of completion so that you can review your progress, show people what you are working on, solicit feedback, and remind yourself of the big picture that ties together the tasks you need to complete. If you are working on an installation painting, sculpture, or other project that is too big to file, consider using a picture or sketch instead. If your assignment is a speech or musical performance, you may want to keep a recording of a recent practice session in your file.

Project outline: If you are working on a presentation or paper, your outline is the roadmap toward your final draft. Keep a copy handy to guide your research and writing.

Task cards: Your task cards summarize the major milestone, tentative due date, and approximate completion time for each task. Task cards should be in chronological order based on their tentative due date. Keep your deck of task cards in the front of your project file. The first card in the deck should be the task you are currently working on. When you finish the task, write the completion date under the tentative due date and move the card to the back of the deck. Use a rubber band or large binder clip to keep your task cards neat and in order.

Notes: Whether you use index cards, a notebook, or loose paper, keep your notes together in your project file so you can refer back to them while you work.

How you store your project file depends on what you need to include and your study habits. If you complete most of the work for your project on a desktop computer, you may find it convenient to keep your project file in a box that you can set by the monitor or under the keyboard. If you work on a laptop, you may prefer to keep your materials in a large laptop bag with your computer. If you are working on a presentation or experiential project that requires many small parts, an organizer bag or toolbox may be a better choice. For projects that generate large amounts of paperwork, a briefcase or portable hanging file box may be useful. If you need to transport your project materials to different work areas, make sure your storage container is portable.

You do not need to spend a lot of money on a storage container for your project file. If money is an issue, do not feel you need to purchase a new, fancy, professional-style organizer from the local office supply store. Many common household objects can pull double-duty as project storage. You may already own some of these possible containers.

Clothes hamper: The shallow, lidless ones are sturdy and easy to move from place to place.

Packing box: Flat, dry materials such as papers and books can be stacked neatly in an ordinary cardboard box. If you will be moving the file or storing heavy loads, consider reinforcing the bottom of the box with strapping tape.

Suitcase: If you do not plan to travel until after you turn your project in, consider keeping your file in a suitcase. A wheeled suitcase can be handy if you need to transport your material. A large one can be used to store parts for an experiential project.

Shopping bags: If you need to keep several oddly shaped objects sorted by color, size, or type, plastic shopping bags are inexpensive choices. Write a description of the contents on each bag using permanent markers or adhesive labels. Be sure to keep your bags where they will not be mistaken for trash.

Decorative containers: If your basement or closet is a graveyard for containers leftover from holiday decorations, flower arrangements, or fruit baskets, you may be able to recycle some of the baskets or bowls into attractive project organizers. Be sure to clean the containers thoroughly to get rid of any dust or chemical residue that may stain your materials.

Desk or dresser drawer: If you do not need a portable container, designate a drawer in your work area to store your material.

Whatever you use to house your project file, make sure to keep the material organized. Do not allow any paper, book, or tool not related to the project to find its way into the file. Keep the materials you need for the current task at the top of the file. After you finish a task, take out the materials you will not need anymore.

Tip 37: Stay motivated.

To complete a large project successfully, you need to work consistently over a period of days, weeks, or months. One way to stay enthusiastic about the assignment and motivated to work as well as you can at every study session is to reward yourself when you reach certain intermediary goals.

You may want to reward yourself for every five or 10 work sessions. Another idea is to get a treat for reaching each major milestone that you defined in the project schedule. However you decide to divide the project, promise yourself rewards that you will look forward to receiving and that will encourage you to continue progressing.

A reward does not have to be expensive or time consuming. For many students, the best motivations are symbolic rituals at the end of a work session or milestone. Some ideas to keep your enthusiasm high include:

A square of fancy chocolate: You may want to count out enough for each milestone on your schedule and keep the squares on top of your desk. As you watch the number of chocolates dwindle, you will have visual confirmation that the project is nearly complete.

A special calendar: If you ceremoniously mark the days you work on the project with a bright red X on a wall calendar or planner, you can keep track of how much time you have invested in the assignment. Looking back over the series of work sessions may help you feel accomplished and motivate you to continue.

A progress blog: Share your accomplishments by posting descriptions and photographs online. You may want to record your ideas and suggestions for future projects, too.

A project buddy: Give a copy of your project schedule to a friend or family member. Keep them apprised of your progress. Discuss your successes and setbacks. A project buddy gives you someone to be accountable to and someone to act as a sounding board to work through ideas with.

A master chart: You are never too old to enjoy a gold star. Make a chart of the project tasks and place a sticker next to each milestone after you complete it. Post your chart on the wall by your work area, on your project file container, or in the front of your project notebook so it is easy for you to see how much progress you have made.

A day off: If your schedule will allow it, give yourself a rest day after you reach a major milestone. Occasional breaks give you something to look forward to, and they can also help you recharge and approach subsequent phases of your project with more energy and creativity.

Whatever reward strategy you choose, try to face each new task and milestone with enthusiasm instead of dread.

Tip 38: Choose and use your references wisely.

For many long-term assignments, the sources you use will be a major factor in the quality of your final product. If you do not use informative and accurate books, articles, and interviews, the conclusions you draw may be factually or logically flawed.

WHERE TO FIND SOURCES

The first step in finding a source is to think about what kind of references you need. The basic types of references include:

Books: For many types of project, the first place to look for information is in books about the topic.

Short stories: If you are working on a project about an author or literary period, you may need to read short stories related to your topic. Short stories may be gathered in anthologies or published in periodicals.

Newspaper articles: Newspapers are daily or weekly publications that contain stories about news of interest to residents of a certain geographic area.

Magazine articles: Magazines are collections of articles and stories that are published on a periodic schedule, such as weekly, monthly, or every other month. Magazines are designed to be casual reading for a broad market.

Journal articles: Journals are periodicals that are written for an audience that already has a certain level of knowledge about the subject. Journals are more scholarly than magazines.

Audio recordings: If you are working on a music project or preparing for a performance, you may need to research audio recordings.

Television shows and movies: News shows, documentaries, and televised interviews can be project sources. Even comedies, dramas, and reality television shows may be useful for some social studies or popular culture topics.

Interviews: A personal discussion with a scholar, or someone who lived through an event, can add color to your project and give you a chance to ask questions about parts of the topic that you do not understand.

Lectures: You may be able to use direct quotes or factual information from a lecture given by an expert on the subject of your project.

Web sites: Colleges, government agencies, private individuals, and corporations may have information you can use for your project available over the Internet.

Plays: Live plays can serve as inspiration sources for your own dramatic performance. If you are preparing a project on a playwright or specific type of literature, scripts can give you examples of characteristic imagery, syntax, character development, and plot devices.

The types of sources you need will depend on the kind of project you are working on, the topic you are researching, and the assignment requirements. If your teacher lists a minimum number of articles, books, or interviews that should be used for project, make sure you follow the guidelines.

Before adding a reference to your working bibliography, ask the following questions:

Is it relevant? Look for references that are closely related to the topic of your project, not ones that you can pull a single extraneous quote from.

Is the material biased? A book, article, or interviewee that approaches the topic of your project with prejudice may be a useful reference if you recognize the bias and present subjective information as opinion, not fact.

Is the material up-to-date? Subjects such as science, global politics, and technology change rapidly. Older sources may not give an accurate picture of current knowledge and situations. Check for new editions of books or articles that are more recent. If you must use an outdated source, confirm the status of countries, cities, theories, and processes before you compose the final draft of your project.

Is the information verifiable? Before accepting your source material as fact, make sure other references agree with the information.

Is the source reliable? Use information from publishers or experts that are respected in a subject related to your project. Your neighbor with a Ph.D. in civil engineering may be a good source for a science project about modular construction, but not for your paper on Ernest Hemingway. If you use a Web site, make sure the information you use comes from a business, school, agency, or individual with appropriate credentials.

Can you cite the source material? If you are not able to add the reference to your bibliography, look for an alternate source. Avoid using information that you remember reading somewhere or that you consider common knowledge.

What is the material's reputation among experts in the field? If you are looking for musical recordings to use as inspiration for your own performance, look for compact discs that were lauded by critics. These may be different from the most commercially successful versions of the piece.

Where to Find Project Sources		
Books	Libraries Personal Collections	Books that are timely, relevant to your project topic, and written by experts with no agendas
Books, cont.	Bookstores Online book retailers	For fiction, look for recent or well-regarded editions
Stories	Anthologies Periodicals Web sites	Stories that are closely related to the topic of your project
Newspaper articles	Libraries Newspaper archives Online news portals	Articles that are nonbiased or opinion pieces where the writer's point of view is explicitly stated For national or international events, newspapers that are highly regarded and well known
Magazine articles	Libraries Personal collections Magazine archives	
Journal articles	Libraries Personal Collections Journal archives	Articles closely related to your topic Articles in peer-reviewed journals Articles that you understand completely
Audio recordings	College or conservatory music libraries Music retailers Radio station listings Radio station archives	Good quality recordings Critically acclaimed performances Recordings of pieces you are preparing
Television shows and movies	Television guides Television station archives Private collections Libraries Retailers	Timely and accurate shows Documentaries that are not commercials for a company or political position Verifiable information

Where to Find Project Sources		
Interviews	College and university faculties Private industry	Eyewitnesses to historical events Experts on a related subject
Interviews, cont.	Nonprofit organizations Government agencies	Authors of books and articles related to your project topic Research investigating problems related to your project topic
Lectures	College and university classes Guest speakers at museums, schools, and nonprofit organizations	Eyewitnesses to historical events Experts on a related subject Authors of books and articles related to your project topic Research investigating problems related to your project topic
Web sites	Internet search engines Online encyclopedias Links from other Web sites	Web sites affiliated with colleges or government agencies Web sites written by experts on a subject related to your project topic Web sites referenced by journal articles or books Web sites that cite their sources Web sites with accurate and verifiable information
Plays	Libraries Schools Professional theaters Community theaters Art academics	Productions of plays you are studying or preparing to perform Plays written by a writer you are researching Plays written in a literary period you are researching Plays written in a style or using a device you are researching

If you need or would like to interview someone for your project, ask your teacher, neighbors, friends, and parents for potential experts or eyewitnesses. You may be surprised how many contacts your acquaintances have. If you cannot find someone appropriate, search the Internet, call the appropriate academic department at a nearby college or university, or contact a business or nonprofit organization involved in work related to your project topic. When asking for an interview from an expert or eyewitness to a historical event, take into account the following:

When you contact a potential interviewee, let them know how you found their contact information.

If you do not know who at a school, business, or organization would be a good person to ask to interview, talk to the secretary or receptionist. Explain who you are and what you are researching. Ask for a recommendation about who in the department might have the time, inclination, and expertise to talk with you.

When asking for an interview, be prepared to talk about your project and what information you will need from the interviewee. Know about how long the interview will take.

Schedule the interview at a time and location that is convenient for your interviewee.

Remember that the interviewee is doing you a favor. Thank them for scheduling the interview.

Show up for the interview on time, professionally dressed, and prepared to take notes or record the interviewee's responses.

Do not let the interview run over the time you arranged when asking for the interview.

After the interview, send a thank you note expressing your appreciation for the interviewee's time. Once your project is finished, send the interviewee a copy.

As you search for an interviewee, a professor, student, or administrator may mention an upcoming lecture about a topic related to your project. If you would like to attend a lecture given as part of a college course, be sure to ask the lecturer first. Once you have permission to attend, follow these guidelines:

- Ask if there is any material you should review before attending the lecture. Make sure you complete any preparations the lecturer recommends.

- Arrive at the lecture hall or classroom a few minutes early. Introduce yourself to the lecturer and ask if there is a particular place you should sit.

- Try not to interrupt the class or inconvenience the students or lecturer.

- Ask for permission before you tape the lecture.

- If you have questions about the lecture, wait until after the class and ask the lecturer for an interview. Do not force the lecturer to spend class time talking about material that might have been covered earlier in the course.

- Even if you are taping the lecture, take notes about interesting quotes and information that relates to your project.

- Write down the time, date, and place of the lecture in addition to the lecturer's name and course catalog number. If you use the lecture as a source for your project, you will need the information for your list of works cited.

- After the lecture, take a moment to thank the lecturer.

QUOTING SOURCES

When writing a paper or documenting a presentation, performance, or experiential project, you may need to document where a quote or fact comes from. Citing your sources allows readers to verify the accuracy of your information and know where to go if they would like to learn more.

Your teacher may expect you to cite your sources for direct quotations, paraphrases, and summaries. Direct quotations are statements in your project that you copied word for word from a book, lecture, interview, or other source. If you reword information from a source without significantly changing the number of words used to present the information, you have paraphrased the source. A summary is a condensation of information from a source written in your own words. The following shows examples of direct quotes, paraphrases, and summaries.

Examples of Ways to Use Sources
Source Material
Ichthyophthirius multifiliis, commonly known as "ich," is a common disease among freshwater fish. Aquarium owners should always be on the lookout for the tell-tale white spots that look like grains of sugar on the fishes' fins, tails, and scales. If it is detected and treated early, ich does not have to be fatal. However, even a slight case of ich can weaken a fish's immune system and put it at risk for secondary infection.
Ich may not be completely preventable, but certain practices can decrease the chance of an outbreak. Buy fish and plants only from reputable dealers. Before purchasing a fish, examine it and the other fish in its tank for signs of ich. Quarantine any new fish before adding them to an established tank.
Direct Quote
"Aquarium owners should always be on the lookout for the tell-tale white spots that look like grains of sugar on the fishes' fins, tails, and scales."

Examples of Ways to Use Sources

Paraphrase

Freshwater fish are susceptible to Ichthyophthirius multifiliis, a disease that leaves visible white granules on infected fishes' bodies. Untreated, I. multifiliis can be fatal. The disease can also lead to secondary infections.

Aquarium owners can reduce the likelihood of I. multifiliis in their fish by taking protective measures when introducing new fish to their tanks. Aquarists should consider the reputation of the dealer and inspect the tank for the I. multifiliis before choosing a new fish. After a fish is purchased, quarantine procedures should be followed to help protect the tank population.

Summary

Ichthyophthirius multifiliis, or "ich," can be treated if the distinctive white grains are caught early. Taking extra care when selecting and adding new fish to an existing tank can help reduce the chance of an outbreak.

Plagiarism is the failure to clearly show where a statement, quote, or idea came from. To avoid charges of plagiarism, you should reveal the source of all direct quotes, paraphrases, and summaries. When citing a source, you also need to be clear about how much of your writing is drawn from the reference material. The table below gives an example of an ambiguous citation and a suggestion for making the source of the material clearer.

Examples for Ambiguous and Clear Citations

Source Material:

Traditional Irish music is conventionally taught without the aid of sheet music. Some musicians believe that the aural traditional continues because it is the best way to help students develop timing, intonation, and phrasing skills. Others point out that the convention was born out of practicality, since few folk musicians of the past were able to read music fluently, and continues only because it offers a nostalgic link to the past.

Ambiguous Citation

For years, musicians have learned traditional Irish tunes not by reading sheet music but by listening to other players. One possible reason for this custom is that it is considered the best way for students to learn technique and interpretation. Another possible reason is that not many traditional players of the past could read music (Stoddard 82).

Examples for Ambiguous and Clear Citations

Problem

The reader cannot know how much of the text came from the source material. It is impossible for the reader to know if the citation refers to the entire paragraph or just the last sentence.

Clear Citations

According to Brook Stoddard, past generations of musicians learned traditional Irish tunes not by reading sheet music but by listening to other players. One possible reason for this custom is that it is considered the best way for students to learn technique and interpretation. Another possible reason is that not many traditional players of the past could read music (82).

CITING YOUR SOURCES

There are three commonly used ways to cite a source: parenthetical citations, endnotes, and footnotes. Be sure to follow the style your teacher requires.

Parenthetical citations: The Modern Language Association (MLA) suggests enclosing key information that identifies the source in parentheses after the cited information. For books, the information is the author's last name and the page number where the information can be found.

Endnotes: To reference your sources using endnotes, mark each direct quote, paraphrase, or summary with a superscript number, then list the proper citations at the end of the paper with the corresponding number.

Footnotes: Like endnotes, footnotes are made by tagging each direct quote, paraphrase, or summary with a superscript number. The citations are then gathered at the bottom, or foot, of each page of the paper, organized by the superscript number.

Each citation should give enough information that a reader should be able to use your list of works cited to see what source you used to write the passage and find the referenced material in the source. For books and articles, the parenthetical citation would include the author's last name and the page number. If you mention the author's name at beginning of the passage, you would only need to add the page number at the end. If you cite two works by the same author, differentiate between the sources by using an abbreviation of the title in the citation.

Footnotes and endnotes include more bibliographic information than parenthetical citations. Most word processing programs have tools to make creating and formatting footnotes and endnotes simple and quick.

The following table compares the three citation formats, demonstrating how each one is used in a paper.

Citation Formats		
Situation	MLA Parenthetical Citation	Endnote/Footnote
Book by one author, information is found on page 44	(Moore 44)	[1] Adrienne Moore, <u>Creating an Aquarium Waterscape</u> (New Orleans: Underwater Press, 2007) 44.
Book by two authors, information found on page 127	(Keller and Blaine 127)	[2] Astrid Keller and Howard Blaine, <u>Basic Chemistry for the Freshwater Tank Novice</u> (London: Peacock Publishing, 1998) 127.
Magazine article, information on page 16	(Marcher 16)	[3] Paul Marcher, "An Insider's Look at Goldfish Breeding," <u>The Freshwater Aquarium Hobbyist</u> 20 Dec. 2003: 16.

CREATING A LIST OF WORKS CITED

One of the most common bibliography forms used for high school projects is the MLA style. The following table shows how to format the bibliographic entries for some common types of sources you may cite in your project using MLA style.

Bibliographic Entries in MLA Style	
Situation	Example
Book with one author	Moore, Adrienne. Creating an Aquarium Waterscape, New Orleans: Underwater Press, 2007.
Book with two authors	Keller, Astrid, and Howard Blaine. Basic Chemistry for the Freshwater Tank Novice. London: Peacock Publishing, 1998.
Book with three authors	Miller, Louis R., Sylvia Hinkle, and Maxwell B. Arthur. Bring the Pond Indoors: Techniques for a Naturalized Tank. Seattle: Pet Press, 2000.
Book with more than three authors	Smith, Patrick R., et al. The Aquarist's Life. New York: Pentagon Press, 2008.
Book by an organization or business	International Freshwater Aquarium Enthusiasts Association. A Beginner's Guide to Purchasing a Freshwater Aquarium. Columbus: IFAEA, 2005.
Article from a weekly or monthly publication	Marcher, Paul. "An Insider's Look at Goldfish Breeding." The Freshwater Aquarium Hobbyist 20 Dec. 2003: 15-17.
Multiple works by the same author	Walsh, Ingrid. Aquarium Fish and Foliage. New York: Vision Press, 2005. --, Breeding Freshwater Species in Captivity. Seattle: Pet Press, 2007.
Recording	Dakota, Polly. Whale Songs of the Northeast Revisited, Compact Disc. Nature Sounds, 1234-90b, 2001.
Movie	The Underwater World, Dir. Michelle Simone, Natural World Productions, 1989.
Interview	Daniels, Alex. Personal interview. 7 Feb. 2008.
Web site	IFAEA Homepage. Ed Phillip Cord, 2008. International Freshwater Aquarium Enthusiasts Association. 8 Feb. 2008 <http://www.samplesite.com>.

Bibliographic Entries in MLA Style	
Document from a Web site	Ray, Julie. "Setting Up Your First Aquarium." IFAEA Homepage, Ed Phillip Cord. 2008. International Freshwater Aquarium Enthusiasts Association. 8 Feb. 2008 <**http://www.samplesite.com/page1**>.
Lecture	Morgan, Bertha. Class lecture, Biology 274. Walsh Creek Community College, Walsh Creek, TN. 8 Jan. 2008.

When you use the MLA style to list the bibliographic information for an article, the page number where the article is found in the publication is the last piece of information in the entry. Entries for recordings include the name of the artist, title of the recording, type of medium, manufacturer, catalog number, and year of release.

If you use MLA to format your paper, arrange the bibliographic entries in alphabetical order by the first word of the entry, ignoring the words "the," "an," and "a," as in the following example.

Example List of MLA Style
Dakota, Polly. Whale Songs of the Northeast Revised. Compact Disc. Nature Sounds, 1234-90b, 2001.
Daniels, Alex. Personal interview. 7 Feb. 2008.
IFAEA Homepage. Ed. Phillip Cord. 2008. International Freshwater Aquarium Enthusiasts Association. 8 Feb. 2008 <**http://www.samplesite.com**>.
International Freshwater Aquarium Enthusiasts Association. A Beginner's Guide to Purchasing a Freshwater Aquarium. Columbus: IFAEA, 2005.
Keller, Astrid, and Howard Blaine. Basic Chemistry for the Freshwater Tank Novice. London: Peacock Publishing, 1998.
Keyes, Marcia. "Fins and Friends at Weekend's Goldfish Convention." Pinewood Daily Register 12 June 2007: B4.

Example List of MLA Style

Miller, Louis R., Sylvia Hinkle, and Maxwell B. Arthur. Bring the Pond Indoors: Techniques for a Naturalized Tank. Seattle: Pet Press, 2000.

Marcher, Paul. "An Insider's Look at Goldfish Breeding." The Freshwater Aquarium Hobbyist 20 Dec. 2003: 15-17.

Moore, Adrienne. Creating an Aquarium Waterscape. New Orleans: Underwater Press, 2007.

Morgan, Bertha. Class lecture. Biology 274. Walsh Creek Community College, Walsh Creek, TN. 8 Jan. 2008.

Ray, Julie. "Setting Up Your First Aquarium." IFAEA Homepage. Ed. Phillip Cord. 2008. International Freshwater Aquarium Enthusiasts Association. 8 Feb. 2008 <**http://www.samplesite.com/page1**>.Smith, Patrick R., et al. The Aquarist's Life. New York: Pentagon Press, 2008.

The Underwater World. Dir. Michelle Simone. Natural World Productions, 1989.

Walsh, Ingrid. Aquarium Fish and Foliage. New York: Vision Press, 2005.

---. Breeding Freshwater Species in Captivity. Seattle: Pet Press, 2007.

The MLA periodically updates its bibliography standards. For information about the most current practices, visit **www.mla.org**.

If you are required to use a format other than MLA, check with your school or local library for the appropriate style guide.

Tip 39: Plan to finish early.

In addition to starting your project early, plan to finish it before the due date. For example, if your teacher assigns a paper that will be due in four weeks, consider setting a project schedule that will have you printing your final draft after only three weeks. Finishing a major project early can have many benefits.

Less stress: If you create a work schedule that allows you to finish a week or two before you turn the assignment in, you do not have to go into panic mode if you are late finishing a major milestone.

More chances to be creative: You may find that your best ideas occur a day or two after you turn your project in. Finishing the assignment early will give you time to incorporate last minute ideas or give your work an extra polish.

Time to ask for help: Have someone look over your work for grammar, stylistic, or logical mistakes. Teachers or classmates are more likely to agree to review and critique your work if they can look over your project at their convenience. If you finish your work early, you will not have to rush potential proofreaders.

A chance for a break before the last step: By the time you reach the final milestone of your project, you may feel burnt out and bored by the topic and process. If you are on track to finish well before the assignment due date, you are more likely to be able to take a day or two off toward the end of your work schedule. Just a day or two away from the project may be enough to let you approach the remainder of your work with more focus and enthusiasm.

Finish your project early as possible, but be careful not cut yourself so short on time that you sacrifice the quality of your work.

CONQUER YOUR DEMONS

People can be their own worst enemies when it comes to academic success. Commitment, attitude, concentration, and self-image issues can keep you from working at your highest level of potential.

By recognizing the internal factors that may be affecting your scholastic performance and taking steps to bring down those barriers, you can make each study session more productive.

Tip 40: Determine what is keeping you from succeeding.

Even students who always tend to have the highest test grades and class rankings have subjects they find difficult. The student who flies through a calculus assignment might panic at the thought of a science project. A student who can pick up foreign languages quickly might dread sitting down for a geography test.

An academic weakness is a subject or kind of assignment that is a substantial challenge to an individual. For many students, academic weaknesses are not the result of innate talents or genetic ability. Instead, they are the product of artificial barriers to success. By understanding what issues stand between you and success, you will be in a better position to cross those barriers and conquer your academic barriers. The following worksheet can help you see what issues may be holding you back.

Identifying Barriers to Your Success

Put a checkmark beside the statements that describe you.

1. It seems like I am always thinking about something else while I am doing my homework.

2. It does not matter if I pay attention in class or not. I can pick up the information I need from reading the textbook or someone else's notes.

3. I am one of those people who is just not very good with numbers.

4. I do not understand the information until someone explains it to me one-on-one.

5. I am sure I can do the work; I just have trouble getting started.

6. The moment I turn an assignment in, I start to worry about what grade I will get.

7. I seldom raise my hand in class, especially if I do not understand the material that is being discussed.

8. I never do well in language arts classes.

9. As soon as I start my homework, I think of a something else that is more important to do.

10. I can work toward my academic goals for a few days, but then I tend to fall back into my usual study patterns.

11. If I get a bad grade, I shove the paper in my book or backpack before anyone can see it.

12. I like to listen to music or watch television while I study.

13. Occasionally a teacher will make a statement or show a diagram that clears up all the questions I had about a concept.

14. The information I learn in school will not be relevant to me in the "real world."

Identifying Barriers to Your Success

15. When I take a test, I get so nervous that I forget information I know I studied.

16. I spend a lot of time planning projects, but I lose interest when it is time to do the work.

17. I am not very good at school.

18. I understand material better after watching a demonstration or doing an experiment.

19. If I do not enjoy an assignment, I wait until the last minute to work on it.

20. Most of my notes and assignments are covered with doodles.

21. Most of my school assignments are boring.

22. I worry a lot about what people think about me.

23. I will not miss my favorite television show to study for a test.

24. The night before a big test, I have trouble relaxing enough to fall asleep.

Interpreting Your Answers

Numbers Checked	Possible Barriers
1, 12, or 20	**Poor concentration:** The amount of time you invest in studying is not as important as the amount of work you complete. If you catch yourself daydreaming while staring at your textbook, poor concentration may be keeping you from reaching your academic potential.
2, 14, or 21	**Bad attitude:** Students who walk into a classroom convinced that they know more than the teacher or that the class will be a waste of their time are sabotaging their own success.
3, 8, or 17	**Poor self-image:** If you believe you are bad at a subject or activity, you may be holding yourself back from making improvements.
4, 13, or 18	**Suboptimal presentation:** It can be difficult to process information if the material is not presented in a way that works for your personal learning style. For example, tactile learners who study for a test only by reading the textbook may not be learning as much as they would if they used flap books, slide cards, and other targeted techniques. Students with learning disabilities may need to see or hear information differently than it is given in class.

Interpreting Your Answers	
Numbers Checked	**Possible Barriers**
5, 9, or 19	**Procrastination:** A carefully constructed study schedule is useless if a student keeps choosing other activities over schoolwork. Putting off tasks seldom has long tem benefits.
6, 15, or 24	**Anxiety:** Anxiety stems from putting too much pressure on one's self to do well at a task. Students who are anxious about exams, performances, or grades may define success by how other people judge the quality of their work, not by their own satisfaction.
7, 11, or 22	**Fear:** Some students are afraid of how other people will react if they ask a question in class, perform in a play, or give a presentation. They may be afraid of their parents' reaction to a test grade or a college admittance committee's judgment about an application. Fear holds people back from trying their best. Even if they do attempt to move outside their comfort zone, fear may keep people from focusing one hundred percent of their effort on success. That way, they can justify failure with the knowledge that they did not try that hard.
10, 16, or 23	**Lack of commitment:** Many students would like to do well on a test or write a brilliant term paper, but few are willing to commit the time and make the sacrifices needed to succeed.

Once you recognize the obstacles between you and scholastic success, you may decide to take one of the following actions:

Seek out help: Your school, parents, the Internet, and this book may be able to guide you to resources that can help you change your work habits.

Create a strategy: Think of improving your study habits as a project, just like a term paper or science project. The same project management skills you use to plan large assignments can help you break down your academic barriers.

Make a change: Recognizing a problem often provides the motivation to make academic improvements.

Ignore the problem: Some students may find it difficult to accept any responsibility for their academic progress. They would rather invent a series of excuses for poor performance than attack the core of the problem.

If you decide to take action against your academic barriers, the tips in this chapter can give you the information and inspiration you need to move forward.

Tip 41: Make boring subjects fun.

If you find a particular class, assignment, or subject challenging, you may find yourself in a self-feeding cycle. For example, if a student finds math difficult, he may find it frustrating and tedious to do his math assignments. Because he does not enjoy it, he rushes through his math work and gets poor grades on the test. The poor grades confirm what he has already convinced himself of — he is just not good at math.

In this example, the cycle could be broken if the student devoted more time to completing his math assignments and learning the material. Many people find it hard to spend time in activities they consider boring or unpleasant. If you are trying to conquer a challenging subject, using the following strategies might help.

During each study session, work on your least favorite subject first. If you put it off until last, you may spend the entire session filled with dread or moving slowly so that you run out of time before you have to face your most challenging work.

Give yourself something to look forward to. Make the time you work on your least favorite tasks the most pleasant minutes of your day. Indulge in your favorite tea. Wrap yourself up in a cozy quilt. Turn on a special lamp or light a fragrant candle. Develop a ritual that will help you relax before you start working on your challenging subject.

Ask questions. If you do not understand the material, odds are good that someone else in the class is lost, too. Ask your teacher to clarify any concepts that are not clear. Arrange for help outside class if necessary.

Set goals. Try to work on the challenging subject a certain amount of time per study session. If you finish your assignment before your allotted time is up, use the extra minutes to review previous work or read upcoming material.

Reward yourself. After you meet a study goal, treat yourself to a small motivational treat.

Seek out victories. Look for ways to improve your confidence in the subject matter. For example, you may want to read a textbook a grade or two below your current skill level, take a non-academic class in a related subject through your local adult education program, or read a non-technical book about the subject. During your study session, work out the examples in your textbook and problems that look easier than the ones your teacher assigned.

Become your own cheerleader. When you sit down with challenging material, tell yourself that you are good at that subject. If you are stuck on a problem, remind yourself that you can do it. Have faith in your abilities and perseverance.

Take a break. If you are stuck on a problem or concept, take a break and come back to it later. Do not let yourself become so frustrated that you fall into a negativity loop.

Join a group. Check to see if your school or community sponsors a social group that focuses on your challenging subject. By joining a science club, French society, or writing group, you may have the opportunity to learn from people who truly enjoy the subject.

If there is a subject you do not enjoy, take steps to make the time you spend working on that subject more interesting and fun.

Tip 42: Do not accept other people's excuses for you.

If you are already uncertain about your ability to succeed in a particular class or with an assignment, your doubt may be cemented if a friend, teacher, or parent gives you the right excuse. Some confidence-busting excuses you might hear include:

- "I was never very good in that class, either."

- "Many kids your age have trouble with that."

- "Your teacher should not have assigned something that hard."

- "That class is not important."

- "You will not need to know that in the real world."

- "No one in our family can do that, either."

- "Not everyone is cut out for school."

- "I never learned that and it never held me back."

- "I think that is too advanced for you."

There are many reasons other people may excuse your academic challenges. For example:

- ❧ They may think they are showing sympathy and helping you feel better.

- ❧ They may have performed badly at something similar and feel insecure at the thought of your success.

- ❧ If they are good at a particular subject, they may want to maintain a sense of superiority.

- ❧ They may not think you are capable of doing the work.

- ❧ No matter what the motivation, hearing these statements gives students excuses to stop trying their hardest.

If someone close to you is giving you excuses not to succeed, you can handle the situation several ways. You may choose to:

- ❧ Ignore the excuses and work to prove them wrong.

- ❧ Explain that the statements are not helping, even if they are meant to be supportive.

- ❧ Accept the excuses as fact.

How you handle the excuses from other people depends on your motivation level, the motivation of the speaker, and your relationship with the speaker. If a teacher or school administrator makes statements connecting your academic performance with gender, race, nation of origin, sexuality, income, or social status, talk to your parents or a teacher about how to make your school a more supportive environment and nondiscriminatory.

Tip 43: Set reasonable goals.

Whether you are trying to improve your attitude or conquer your fear of exams, it is hard to change habits and develop new behaviors. It may be helpful to create concrete goals related to your academic barriers. Avoid goals that are open-ended, such as "I will work harder at chemistry." Try to write your goals so you can easily tell when you have accomplished them.

You may want to add a time element to your goals. For example, you may try to work on your Spanish vocabulary list for 10 minutes each day until the next test. Avoid making your goals too difficult. It may not be possible to elevate your calculus grade from a D to an A in a month. However, you may be able to improve your understanding of the material and start raising your grade by working toward a goal of completing five extra problems each day during that month.

How you construct your goals is a major factor in how effective they will be toward helping you overcome your academic challenges. The following table contrasts the characteristics of ineffective goals to goals most likely to help move you toward academic success.

Characteristics of Effective and Ineffective Goals		
Ineffective Goals	**Effective Goals**	**Explanation**
Thought About	Written down	Goals that you only think about and try to store mentally are more likely to be forgotten.
Open-ended	Concrete	Students are more likely to abandon open-ended goals because they will not be able to tell when the goals are completed. With a concrete goal such as "Start homework as soon as I get home from school every day for a month," students know when they have completed the goal and should set a new one.

Characteristics of Effective and Ineffective Goals		
Vague	Clear	It can be difficult to know how to start working toward a vague goal such as "become a better music theory student." A clear goal like "review music theory flashcards everyday before class" provides a structure for success.
General	Specific	General goals like "work harder" or "make better grades" can be overwhelming. Focused goals seem more reachable and give a better chance of success.
Unreasonable	Attainable	Goals should be challenging but not feel impossible.

The following chart gives some examples of open-ended goals related to some of the common barriers to academic success discussed in Tip 40. The last column shows how these abstract goals can be rewritten to be more concrete and useful.

Setting Goals to Academic Barriers		
Academic Barrier	**Ineffective Goals**	**Rewritten Goals**
Poor Concentration	Pay more attention in class	• Take notes during every lecture. • Create a list of questions based on the material discussed in class. • Avoid doodling during class until after midterms.
Bad Attitude	Improve self esteem	• Make a progress chart for my most challenging class and give myself a gold star for every homework problem I get right this semester.

Setting Goals to Academic Barriers		
Academic Barrier	**Ineffective Goals**	**Rewritten Goals**
Suboptimal Presentation	Learn about alternative learning techniques and start using techniques geared toward my personal learning style	• Visit the school's language laboratory to listen to German vocabulary words twice a week for the rest of the semester. • Make a flap book for the current history unit and study it before class every day until the test.
Procrastination	Try not to put things off	• Start homework after basketball practice every day for a month.
Anxiety	Relax more	• Do five minutes of yoga at lunch on exam days • Reward myself for preparing for the exam by studying 15 minutes every evening, no matter what grade I receive.
Fear	Care less about other people's opinions	• Audition for the spring musical. • Ask at least one question in class every day of the semester.
Lack of Commitment	Stick to my study plan	• Study for 90 minutes every evening at least four nights a week until midterms.

You may need several steps to conquer your academic barriers. After you reach one goal, review your progress, think about where you would like to improve, and set another target.

Tip 44: Know that you are not alone.

Identifying and overcoming the barriers keeping you from academic success can be a time consuming and even intimidating process. A good support system can help you work toward your goals when you are tired or discouraged with your progress. Your support system may include your:

- Friends
- Parents
- Teachers
- Coaches
- Guidance counselor
- Coworkers
- Teammates
- Extended family members

Not everyone has the disposition to be a good member of your support team. Think about who might be a good person for you to turn to if you need encouragement or advice. Consider the following qualities:

Empathy: Look for people who can understand how you are feeling.

Communication skills: A supporter must be able to listen to what you are saying and put their own feelings into words.

Honesty: Seek out people who will tell you the truth even if it is not what you want to hear.

Trustworthiness: You should feel secure that your supporter will not be talking about your conversations to other people.

Experience: A supporter who has worked through similar issues may be able to give more specific and useful advice.

Observation skills: A good supporter should be able to recognize your strengths and weaknesses.

Self-confidence: Avoid people who may use your discouragement to help bolster their self-esteem.

Technical ability: If you need assistance understanding a concept or assignment, pick a support team member who is skilled in the area where you need help.

Availability: Look for someone who has the time to offer support when you need it.

Expect that each person in your support system will have their own set of talents. When you have a problem or concern, seek out the person who has the best tools to help you. The following worksheet can help you identify people who you might consider support team members.

Building a Support Team	
Directions: Beside each scenario, write the names of two or three people who would be the most likely to give you helpful advice.	
Scenario	**Possible Supporters**
Although you understood the material when your teacher explained it during class, you do not know how to do the assigned problems. You feel frustrated and confused.	
Your English teacher just assigned a large paper. You are convinced that you will not be able to complete the assignment on time.	
You studied hard for a physics test. When the teacher returned it, you were shocked and disappointed by the low grade.	
Your parents just told you that they cannot afford to pay for you to go with the French club to Europe. You are devastated.	
You and your best friend had a huge fight and are not speaking anymore.	
After you made the varsity cross country team, you are finding it hard to adjust to the demands of your new schedule.	
You got a low grade on a computer science quiz and you are afraid to tell your parents.	

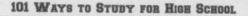

Building a Support Team	
Directions: Beside each scenario, write the names of two or three people who would be the most likely to give you helpful advice.	

Scenario	Possible Supporters
You are preparing for an audition to a prestigious music school. The night before the audition, you are nervous.	
You are interested in science and would like to take an advanced biology class at your school, but you worry that you are not smart enough. You are afraid that you will get the lowest grade on every test.	
You feel left out, lonely, and socially awkward at school.	
You feel like your teacher is singling you out and treating you unfairly.	
You just finished a laboratory report for your chemistry class and need someone to proofread it for you.	
Your journalism teacher assigned you to attend a press conference with a local politician. You are nervous and afraid that you are going to embarrass yourself.	
You suspect you would learn better through tactile learning techniques. You would like to learn more strategies to incorporate in your study sessions.	

Members of your support team are not obligated to help you. You have a responsibility to treat your team members with gratitude and respect. To be a good team leader, keep the following guidelines in mind.

Communicate clearly. Do not assume your support team member knows what you mean. Practice putting your feelings and opinions into words. Listen to what your supporters say verbally and through body language.

Make your intentions known. Be open with your supporter about what you want. If you just need to talk about a problem, you may become annoyed if your team member starts offering advice or solutions. Let people know how if what type of involvement you need from them.

Accept responsibility for yourself. If you take a supporter's advice, you are accountable for the results. Do not be angry with your team member or blame them if the advice does not work out as well as you hoped.

Show your appreciation. Make sure your team members know that you are thankful for the time, energy, and emotional investment that devote to helping you.

Return the favor. There may be times when your team members need support for themselves. Whether they need someone to listen while they talk out a problem, help creating a study schedule, or a critical eye to review an art project, try to find the time to help your supporters and build your relationships.

Tip 45: Use the resources you have available.

If you are having trouble with an assignment, academic subject, or personal issue, you may find help privately, at your school, or through your community. The following table lists some resources you may have available and find useful.

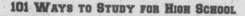

Possible Resources
Private:
Tutoring
Counseling
Online services
School:
Learning center
Study groups
Review sessions
Teacher office hours
Guidance counselor
Library reference material
Community:
Library study hours
Writing groups
Workshops
Continuing education classes
Church groups
Community study halls

Some people have trouble accepting help. They may be afraid that they will look lazy, unmotivated, or incapable if they use school, private, or community resources. Suffering through a problem when there are tools available that may help does not make you smarter or stronger. Using the resources available to you can help save time, frustration, and energy.

Tip 46: Keep a journal.

Identifying and overcoming internal issues that are holding you back can be an emotional process. If you record your successes, difficulties, and feelings in a journal, you can review your progress. Over the course of a semester or school year, you will see where you have improved and what areas still need work.

As you encounter problems, write your ideas for solutions in your journal. Record any actions you took to resolve your issues and your reflections on the outcomes. If you run into similar problems later, you can refer to your journal to see which strategies worked and which flopped.

You can keep your journal in a notebook, binder, diary, or on a computer. What you use as a journal is not as important as what you write. You do not have to bare your soul in your journal, but be sure to record:

- How you prepare for tests

- Ideas for upcoming projects

- Steps you take toward meeting academic and personal goals

- Questions about assignments

- Successful study techniques

- Places where you have noticed improvement

- Areas that still need work

- Goals you want to work toward in the future

You may decide to write in your journal daily, weekly, or whenever the urge strikes you. Be sure to keep your journal accessible to write in and review.

MAKE CLASS TIME COUNT

Your regular study sessions are an opportunity to master information, work on assignments, read new material, and practice skills. They are an important part of succeeding in school and, perhaps more important, learning.

Study sessions are not substitutes for attending and paying attention during class. There are many kinds of learning experiences that may be available to you during class which are difficult to duplicate outside school, including:

Interaction with your teacher: Students who learn better by listening to information can benefit from hearing lectures. By paying attention to what points your teachers emphasize, you will have a clearer idea of what they find important and are most likely to include on tests. Teachers often welcome polite and on-topic questions during class time, so if you are confused about a concept, you can get immediate clarification.

Interaction with other students: Whether you are playing in an orchestra or learning conversational phrases in French, class time offers a convenient opportunity to practice and cooperate with other students.

Guided practice: When you conjugate a verb, complete a geometry proof, or play a scale in class, your teacher and classmates can help diagnose and fix problems. This will help decrease the time you spend trying to understand a technique or practicing incorrect procedures during your study session.

Experience with advanced equipment: Your classroom may be outfitted with equipment and supplies that are not available to you at home. Class time can give you experience with microscopes, shop tools, specialized software, and art supplies that you would otherwise not have access to.

TEACHERS' RESPONSIBILITIES

Although you are ultimately responsible for your education and studying, your teachers have specific duties they need to fulfill to help their classroom function smoothly and their students learn. Teacher responsibilities include:

Arriving for class prepared: Your teacher should have a goal for each class and a plan for meeting that goal.

Returning graded assignments and tests in a timely matter: Corrected homework and exams can help students recognize areas they do not understand. Graded assignments should be returned to students before they are tested on the material so the students have enough time to review concepts they have problems with. All tests should be corrected and returned to students before midterm or final exams that cover the same material.

Stating behavior and academic expectations: Teachers should be clear about what is acceptable in their classroom. Students should be made aware of how late assignments, missed tests, absences, and behavior issues will be handled.

Enforcing rules equally: If some students get full credit for a late assignment and others suffer 10 point penalties, the class is likely to grow frustrated and confused. Teachers should apply their rules uniformly without regard to a student's social status, gender, sexuality, appearance, race, age, or reputation.

Teachers who do not fulfill their responsibilities put their students in awkward positions. If you have a teacher who regularly shows up to class unprepared, returns assignments weeks after they were handed in, creates frivolous rules, or treats certain students unfairly, you may be in a classroom situation that discourages learning. Consider taking one of the following steps to help improve the situation:

- Go directly to the teacher with your concerns. The teacher may not realize there is a problem and may be willing to change the classroom environment after you bring attention to the issue.

- Keep a list of the dates, times, and descriptions of the teacher's questionable behavior.

- Talk to another teacher, a parent, or an administrator about the classroom conditions.

You have a right to learn in an effective classroom. If problems with a teacher continue, you may want to take steps to be moved into another class.

YOUR RESPONSIBILITY TO THE CLASS

The duty to create a successful learning environment does not rest solely on the shoulders of the teachers. Students also have responsibilities to themselves, their teachers, and their classmates. The tips in this chapter can help you learn more during your time in class, which means less study time in the evenings and on weekends. These tips will also help your teacher move through material and create a better learning environment for everyone.

Tip 47: Minimize your absences.

When you are absent from class, you may miss learning new material, watching demonstrations, discussing homework, or practicing concepts. Valuable class time can be wasted if a teacher has to repeat information to the entire class because of a few students who were absent. If the teacher does not take the time to catch students up, they may miss important information.

You may need to miss class because of illness, school activities, or appointments that have to be scheduled during school hours. Do not add to your absence count because of avoidable reasons. Some poor reasons to miss class include:

- You do not what to take a test.

- You have not finished an assignment.

- You want to go on vacation.

- You just do not feel like going to school.

- You want to sleep late.

You do not want to see someone who is going to be at school.

Before missing a day of school, ask yourself the following:

Why am I missing class? Be honest with yourself about your motivation.

Is my condition infectious? Avoid going to school if you are likely to make other people sick.

Is anyone counting on me? If you are part of a group that will be presenting a project that day, your absence may affect several people's grades.

How could I prevent missing class in the future? If you are tempted to stay home from school because you are too tired to get ready, review your schedule and see what changes would help ensure you are well-rested.

How much class time do I have to miss? Even if you have a doctor's appointment that can not be rescheduled, you may be able to attend school for part of the day.

What will you miss? What information will your teachers cover? Will there be any in class activities?

How will you catch up? How will you get the notes and assignments you missed? Do you have enough time available to do the work?

What are the long-term effects of the absence? Your school system, institution, or teachers may have incentives to encourage you to attend class. Find out how your absence will affect your grade and exam schedule.

Excessive absences can nourish the attitude that education is not important. If students do not value their time in school, teachers are less likely to make an effort to keep classes interesting.

Tip 48: Come prepared.

If you want to participate fully and get the most out of each class, just showing up is not enough. You should arrive at class ready to work. In addition to having the tools and supplies you need, you should also have completed any reading or problems your teacher assigned.

If you have trouble coming to class prepared, make a checklist and keep it where you can refer to it easily. It may be helpful to make a different checklist for each class. You may want to keep your checklists in your planner, staple them to the corresponding class notebook, tape them to your locker, or pin them on the wall next to your bedroom door.

Some items you may need to add to your checklists include:

- Textbook
- Notebook
- Homework
- Planner
- Pen
- Pencil
- Calculator
- Dictionary

Tip 49: Practice smart note taking.

Once you are in class, make the most of the time by taking notes on what your teacher says and the type of activities you do. When teachers talk about a concept, do a demonstration, or arrange for an experiential learning activity, the odds are good that they think the concept is important. The ideas your teachers find significant are more likely to show up on quizzes, exams, and assignments.

Take notes even if you know that the information your teacher is talking about is also in the book. The process of writing the material down will help get it in your brain. If the lecture is moving too quickly, write down some key words and fill in the gaps using your textbook and class handbook. Try to review your notes as soon as possible. You will be able to remember more a few hours after class than you will a week later. If you wait too long, your notes may not make much sense.

When you take class notes, you do not have to write down every word that the teacher says. Instead, write down important concepts, definitions, events, lists, examples, and dates. Your class notes should also include any material the teacher writes on the blackboard or shows on an overhead. During class, listen for phrases like the ones below, which may signal that speakers are covering information they consider especially significant:

- "What you need to know is..."

- "The take home message of all this is..."

- "Some of the reasons for this were..."

- "This was a result of..."

- "Be sure to practice this type of problem."

- "A turning point in the situation was..."

- "This is an example of..."

- "The reason this is important..."

- "This relates to..."

- "The causes were..."

- "The key points are..." or "The key point is..."

- "What we are looking for..."

- "To identify this..."

- "The steps you need to take are..."

- "The crucial point is..."

- "This is used for..."

- "For example..."

Try to keep your notes as neat and legible as possible to avoid the frustration of having to decipher your own handwriting. Underline, highlight, or put a star between information that the teacher emphasizes.

Identifying Lecture Details

The following table shows an excerpt of a lecture for a business studies class. Have a parent or friend read the excerpt out loud. On a separate sheet of paper, take notes on what you think are the important elements of the lecture. Compare your notes to the sample notes provided.

Sample Lecture

Business operations can be divided into two types of activities: production and marketing.

Production activities are those things a company does to make a product or perform a service. For a tennis shoe company, production activities would include sewing the shoes and gluing on the soles. For a home cleaning service, production would be traveling to the residences, cleaning the kitchen, and vacuuming the carpets.

Marketing includes everything a business does to find out about consumers' needs and desires, how the business uses this research to guide what the business produces, and the methods the business uses to let consumers know about their products or services. Marketing activities try to connect what the consumer wants to buy with what the business produces. Once the goods are produced, marketing focuses on educating the consumer about how the product matches the consumer's wants and needs.

Marketing activities are just as essential to a business's survival as production. Without marketing, businesses would not be able to produce products or offer services that their customers want, and customers would not know what options were available.

Some examples of marketing activities are advertisements, selling techniques, market analysis, forecasting, and product research. The key point is that these market activities are focused on the company's market. A market is simply everyone who might by the product or use the service. The group of potential customers makes up the market.

So, why is this important to you? As high school students, why should you study marketing? Marketing activity is all around you. The more you learn about the techniques marketers use, the easier it will be for you to recognize the strategies that are employed to try to influence what you choose to purchase. Also, marketing is not limited to large corporations. When you apply for a job, you are trying to get the manager to hire you. You are marketing yourself. If you are selling candy to help pay for a band trip, you can use marketing techniques to help convince your market to buy from you. If you pursue a small business venture, you can use your use of marketing to help differentiate yourself from competitors.

Sample Lecture

For example, you may decide to start a lawn mowing service during summer break. Unfortunately, your next door neighbor had the same idea. If you understand marketing, you could analyze your market and focus on a segment that your neighbor is ignoring. If several of the families in your market are concerned about pollution, for instance, you could offer an environmentally friendly lawn service. Part of your market may be willing to pay more for your service if you use a reel mower instead of a gasoline-powered one.

Your ecologically-friendly lawn service is an example of an important marketing concept called market segmentation. I will define market segmentation in just a moment, but first I want talk about how companies that offer similar products or services may target different markets.

Consider beauty salons. You have your high end shop that charges a small fortune for a haircut, and the inexpensive place where you do not even have to make an appointment. You just walk in, put down your $5 and get a trim. These two businesses offer the same service. They both cut hair. There may be differences in quality and prestige, but the basic product is the same.

Even though they are the same type of business, these two salons are not in direct competition with each other. People who go to the high end salon are not going to go to the cheaper place just because they run a certain advertisement or offer a good coupon. People who go to the $5 shop may go to the high end salon for a special occasion, but they are not likely to think it is a good value. The two salons target a different clientele.

This brings up an important concept in marketing called "market segmentation." Market segmentation is the process of dividing up a market into smaller groups. There are several differences that can be used to segment a market. Businesses can look at the age, gender, or location of their potential customers. They might partition the market based on customers' style preferences. For example, one beauty salon might target customers who want conservative styles while another salon focuses on customers who prefer trendier haircuts. Other factors that might segment a market include lifestyle and buying habits.

The reason market segmentation is important is that companies who offer similar products or services are only in direct competition if they are both pursuing the same segment of the market.

You may have formatted your notes differently than the sample, but you should have written down similar key facts.

Sample Notes

Two types of business activities:

1. Production: The process of making a product or performing a service.

2. Marketing: The process of finding out what consumers want or need, directing the production of goods that meet those wants and needs, and informing the consumers about the products.

Marketing includes:

- advertising

- selling techniques

- market analysis

- forecasting

- product research

Market: A group of potential customers.

Why should high school students learn about marketing? 1) Better able to recognize the techniques used on us as consumers. 2) Able to employ marketing techniques in job searches, fundraising sales, and small business ventures (for example, environmentally friendly lawn mowing service).

There are many consumers who buy similar products or use similar services, but not all similar businesses are in direct competition.

Example: Beauty salons – High end salons target different clientele than inexpensive, walk-in shops.

Market segmentation: Dividing a market into smaller groups based on their demographics, preferences, lifestyles, or buying habits.

Similar companies are only in direct competition if they target the same market segment.

A good set of class notes can be a valuable study guide. In addition, the process of taking thoughtful notes will help you stay more attentive during class. Remember that the more you learn in class, the less you need to learn during your evening and weekend study sessions.

Tip 50: Make sure you understand the material.

It can be difficult for even the most conscientious students to pay attention when they do not understand the material being discussed. If you fall behind in a lecture or get stuck on a detail in an in-class assignment, you can tune out for the remainder of the class or you can take steps to bridge the gap that is keeping you from full comprehension. If you choose to opt out of the class, you will likely find yourself spending more time to catch up than you would invest in dealing with the problem right away.

Depending on the class situation, you may find the following strategies helpful if you find yourself confused.

Ask the teacher. The most likely person to clear up any uncertainty is your teacher. Be sure to ask your question as politely and clearly as possible. Avoid putting your teacher on the defensive with statements like "you have really confused me," or "you switched gears too fast." Instead, make your questions focused and to the point. For example, if you became confused when your teacher jumped from talking about the Boston Massacre to the Amistad trial, ask about the connection between the two events.

Ask a neighbor. If you are working with a partner or small group on an in-class activity, a classmate may be able to explain the challenging concept in a way that you are better able to understand. If other students are also confused, consider asking your teacher to cover the material again.

Look back through your notes. If you are working by yourself on an in-class activity, flip through your notebook and see if the material was discussed in a previous lecture.

Use your textbook. Sometimes checking a definition, name, or equation in your textbook can give you enough information to help you catch up.

As you listen to a lecture, watch a demonstration, or participate in class activities, do not be a passive observer. Silently quiz yourself about the material so that you can recognize and deal with problems promptly. The sooner you deal with comprehension issues, the more you will be able to learn during class.

Tip 51: Help yourself pay attention.

It is easy for teachers and parents to tell you to pay attention during class, but sometimes it can seem impossible to follow that advice. After a long night of studying, the gentle music coming from the band room next door can combine with the warmth from the radiator to make the lure to nap stronger than your best intentions to stay focused while your teacher explains the Pythagorean Theorem.

If you tune out of class, you may be missing information about assignments, material that may show up on tests, or explanations that can help you understand key concepts.

The following tips can help you give yourself the best possible chance to stay attentive during class.

Sit near the action. If your teacher is lecturing, try to find a desk where you can maintain eye contact. During demonstrations and videos, position yourself so you have a good view. If you have to strain to see what it going on, your subconscious may decide that the benefits are not worth the effort.

Sit away from distractions. Find a seat where you will not be tempted to fraternize with classmates, read the bulletin board, gaze at the window, or watch the minute hand on the clock.

Be careful about what you bring to class. Leave erasers, pens, and pencils that have attached toys or other distracting features in your locker. If you find yourself sidetracked by your cell phone, personal digital assistant, mp3 player, or calculator, avoid taking the electronics out of your backpack.

Get a good night's sleep. Give yourself the best possible chance to stay awake during class.

Dress in layers. Taking off your jacket, sweater, or sweatshirt can help stave off the drowsiness that tends to thrive in warm classrooms.

Tip 52: Do not encourage digressions.

Some teachers do not need much coaxing to put away the lesson plan and turn the class into a sermon about current events, their personal life, or problems with the school. When a class gets derailed, you may lose opportunities that could help you master material. The class time that is wasted could be used to:

- Listen to explanations of difficult concepts.

- Ask questions about material that you find confusing.

- Participate in activities that may help you make connections about the subject matter.

- Review homework questions.

🕮 See example of problems you will be expected to solve on exams or assignments.

If a teacher regularly veers off course, consider the following:

🕮 Be patient and keep an open mind. Wait a few minutes before you become too upset about the detour. The teacher may relate seeming digression to the class subject.

🕮 Try to ask questions that relate the conversation to the class subject. For example, if your French class has turned into a debate about gender issues, you might ask about gender roles in France.

🕮 Ask a direct question about a homework assignment.

Do your part to keep the class on task. Avoid asking questions or making comments that you know will lead to a digression. Even though your teachers are being paid to cover pertinent material during school hours, the students are the ones who pay the price when a class routinely becomes a social event or a teacher's soapbox. Do not sabotage your own education.

Tip 53: Organize your notes every day.

Unless you are skilled at shorthand, you may find it difficult to take notes using full sentences and complete thoughts. Depending on how quickly a teacher talks, your writing speed, and how much you need to write down, your class notes might consist of little more than a few keywords and important phrases.

To make your notes as useful as possible, take some time to review and organize them every day. Read over your notes as soon after the class as possible so the material is still fresh in your mind. Use what you have written to jog your memory. Fill in the information that you abbreviated or did not have a chance to write down. If you are confused by something in your notes, try to find the material in your textbook, talk to a classmate, or ask your teacher for clarification.

Type or rewrite your completed notes. Make sure your new notes are in a form that is easy to read.

Completing Class Notes	
Original Notes	**New Notes**
Ion: neg. or pos. atom/molecule Neutral atom/molecule gains/loses a valence electron, makes an ion Anions: ?? Cations: ?? Plasma: group of gas-like ions. Not a solid, gas, or liquid	Ion: an atom or molecule with a negative or positive charge. Ions are formed when a neutral atom or molecule gains or loses a valence electron. Two types of ions: **1. Anions:** Ions with negative charges. An anion is formed when a neutral atom or molecule gains a valence electron. **2. Cations:** Ions with positive charges. A cation is formed when a neutral atom or molecule loses a valence electron. Plasma: A group of gas-like ions. Plasma is not a solid, gas, or liquid.

FOREIGN LANGUAGE STUDY TIPS

Learning a foreign language can present special challenges. You have to memorize vocabulary and conjugations, and will need to learn new grammar and pronunciation rules.

WHY STUDY A FOREIGN LANGUAGE?

There are many reasons you may find a foreign language class on your schedule. Some schools require students to complete one or more units of a foreign language to earn a diploma. Colleges may require applicants to show a level of proficiency in a second language before declaring certain majors.

If you plan on traveling abroad, being able to communicate in the language of your destination country will let you communicate with more people and show respect for the culture. Studying a specific language can also enhance your understanding of other subjects. Biological and medical sciences, for example, use Latin-based terminology. Music uses Italian words to direct speed and volume. Ballet uses French names for movements.

Language courses often cover the history and culture of the countries where the language is spoken, so learning a foreign language can also help you develop a global perspective of current events. Some languages have words or phrases for concepts that are difficult to express in English, so attaining fluency in a foreign language can expose students to new ideas and philosophies.

Common Problems

Learning a foreign language is not always easy. Some languages use sentence structures that would be incorrect if used in English. There may be several words that correspond to a single English word, and articles that change depending on case or tense.

Some languages classify nouns, including inanimate objects, by gender. This can be a difficult concept for native English speakers to understand and master. Even after the rules for gender identification are memorized, there always seem to be exceptions. Students may have trouble pronouncing new sounds or differentiating between sounds that sound similar.

Tip 54: Do not study from the book.

When learning a new language, you may learn vocabulary words and grammar rules more thoroughly in less time if you write the material down instead of reading it from your textbook.

When writing your personal foreign language study guide, keep the following suggestions in mind.

Make sure the material is accurate. Avoid studying mistakes. Check and double check that your spellings, translations, and explanations are correct.

Write it until you know it. If you have trouble remembering a word, phrase, or conjugation, writing the information several times can help you internalize the material.

Keep it simple. Avoid copying every single word in your textbook. Only write what you need to know.

Read out loud as you write. Saying the material while you write will engage all three learning centers: visual, auditory, and tactile. This may help you learn more efficiently.

Neatness counts. If you have trouble reading your own handwriting, you may end up wasting time trying to decipher your study guide during future work sessions.

Make it convenient. Use a form that is portable so you can take your study guide with you and review between classes and activities.

Cater to your personal learning style. If you are a visual learner, paste clip art or sketch images that correspond to your vocabulary words. If you are a tactile learner, make flap books and slide cards. If you are an auditory learner, write words and phrases out phonetically and be sure to read them aloud while you study.

Tip 55: Do not learn vocabulary and conjugations in a vacuum.

Even if your high school language class emphasizes vocabulary lists and grammar exercises, this is not necessarily the best way to learn a language. Some students learn more efficiently when vocabulary and verbs are integrated. This approach better mimics the environment in which children learn their native tongue.

To improve your fluency, take every opportunity you can to combine practicing all element of your new language. Instead of simply listing your verb conjugations, create a sentence using each verb form. Practice vocabulary words by writing dialogues or stories. Your compositions do not have to be complicated to be effective. Build on the vocabulary and sentence structures that you have already mastered.

Tip 56: Try to think in the language as much as possible.

The more you practice your new language, the faster and more thoroughly you will learn. Luckily, language is completely portable. You do not have to wait for class time or your study session to practice. You do not need any special equipment. You can even practice in situations where it would not be appropriate to talk.

Thinking in the language you are studying can help you internalize new words and sentence structures and gives you the opportunity to practice synthesizing your own ideas.

As you walk around your house, use your new language to label the items you see around you. Your thoughts do not have to be complicated. Even sentences like "There is the door" and "I see a cat" can help you gain confidence in your skills.

Tip 57: Seek out opportunities to practice with native speakers.

Speaking with and listening to people who grew up speaking the foreign language you are studying can enhance your learning by giving you:

- Experience picking up a speaker's meaning using the vocabulary you know and the context of the situation

- Encouragement to combine concepts you learned in class in new ways to express your wants and needs

- The opportunity to hear a wider variety of accents and colloquialisms than you are exposed to in class

- Motivation to continue learning by showing the practical applications of mastering the language

Depending on where you live and the language you are studying, finding opportunities to talk with native speakers can be challenging. Some churches sponsor services and social events in foreign languages. Language departments at colleges may host roundtable discussions so native speakers and students can interact. Your teacher may be able to arrange for a practice exchange with a student from another country. In a practice exchange, a pair or small group of people chat in one language for half of the exchange period then switch to another language. That way, each participant practices the language they are learning.

Tip 58: Watch televisions shows and movies in the new language.

Thanks to cable television, satellite broadcasts, and the Internet, students can access television shows, movies, and videocasts from around the world. Watching them can help develop a feel for the pronunciation and contextual comprehension.

You may find it easier to understand what you are watching if you use closed captioning or subtitles. Closed captioning is a running transcription of the show or movie in the language being used. Subtitles translate the dialogue in another language. Watching without captioning or subtitles can help improve your listening comprehension skills.

Tip 59: Read contemporary literature.

An introductory high school language class is likely to cover a limited range of vocabulary. You may learn how to introduce yourself, count, label the furniture in your house, and order from a simple menu. Reading magazines, newspapers, comic books, and novels in the language you are studying can help you learn words and idioms that you would use in every day conversations.

If you are intimidated by the thought of plunging into an article, story, or book armed only with the vocabulary you have learned from class and a dictionary, look for student editions of foreign language writing. These versions are created especially for people learning a new language. They offer features such as side-by-side translations, vocabulary lists, cultural footnotes, and explanations of idioms.

Visual learners may find comic books, cartoons, and graphic novels helpful tools for acquiring vocabulary. Students may also find this type of literature easier to understand because the illustrations can give clues about the meaning of unfamiliar words or phrases. Collections of cartoons with topics of interest to teenagers are available in most major languages. Your teacher may have some suggestions for contemporary illustrated literature that is appropriate for your skill level.

Tip 60: Learn children songs.

Throughout the world, parents teach their preschoolers simple songs and nursery rhymes. These songs are not just fun, they are also aids for learning vocabulary, practicing pronunciation, and forming cultural awareness. Some traditional songs lend themselves well to simple dance movements, and finger play, making them especially useful for tactile learners.

To get the most benefit from learning children's folk songs, find translated versions so you understand what you are singing. Look for books of songs and nursery rhymes at your local library, or search the Internet for specific song titles. The following table can help you find appropriate songs.

Traditional Children's Songs Across the World	
Language	**Song Titles in English**
German	"Abel, Babel, Goose Bill"
	"A Cuckoo Settled on a Tree"
	"A Little Violin"
	"And Who Was Born in January?"
	"Brother James"
	"Chin Tipping"
	"Cuckoo, Cuckoo"
	"Dance, Little Child, Dance"
	"Do You Know How Many Stars There Are?"
	"Good Evening, Good Night"
	"If I Were a Little Bird"
	"Little Rabbit in Your Burrow"
	"My Hat Has Three Corners"
	"The Songs are Sounding"

Traditional Children's Songs Across the World	
Language	**Song Titles in English**
Spanish	"All the Colors" "Five Little Elephants" "I Have a Little Doll" "Jump Over the Board" "Odd and Even Numbers" "Rice with Milk"
French	"A, B, C, D, Some Carrots and Some Turnips" "A Hen on a Wall" "A Little Pig" "At the Clear Fountain" "Brother John" "Colors of Autumn" "Forehead, Little Forehead" "I Love Cake" "In My Boat" "My Hat Has Four Bumps" "One, Two, Three" "Peach, Apple, Pear, Apricot" "The Big Deer" "There Was a Little Ship"
Italian	"As You Sleep in Your Bed" "Butterfly" "Cincirinella" "Clap Your Hands" "Maramao" "Maria is Washing" "Turn, Turn Around"
Russian	"Granny Ate Peas" "Hush, You Mice" "The Horned Goat is Coming" "The Night Has Come"

Traditional Children's Songs Across the World	
Language	**Song Titles in English**
Chinese	"Counting Ducks"
	"Pan and Bottle"
	"Little Swallow"
Japanese	"Cherry Blossoms"
	"Happy Doll Festival"
	"Little Elephant"
	"Moonlight on a Ruined Castle"
	"Rabbit"
	"Rainy Day"
	"Song of Kites"
	"Spring Has Come"

Tip 61: Write in the new language.

There is more to learning how to communicate in a foreign language than memorizing vocabulary lists and grammar rules. Communication is dependent on the ability to express thoughts and feelings in a way that other people can understand.

Writing original compositions in the language you are studying is a way to:

- Explore your creativity: Playing with how words sound and work together can be challenging and fun.

- Practice concepts: The more you use the structures and words you learn in class, the more quickly you will internalize and master the material.

- Broaden your vocabulary: You may need to look up new words to finish your composition.

    ❧   Relate your language studies to other interests: You can write in your new language about any topic.

    ❧   Track your progress: If you keep your compositions in a notebook or in dated files, you can look back over your work and see how your writing has matured as your skills with the language improve.

Some types of pieces you may enjoy writing in a foreign language include:

    ❧   Poems   ❧   Plays

    ❧   Short stories   ❧   Journal entries

    ❧   Essays   ❧   Comics

    ❧   Book reviews   ❧   Greeting cards

    ❧   Song lyrics

Tip 62: Learn from your mistakes.

Pay attention to the red marks on your returned papers. Review any corrections that your teacher makes on your homework, class assignments, or tests. Try not to repeat the mistakes you made. If you duplicate a misspelling or syntax error, you are practicing incorrect material.

If you are writing stories, songs, or dialogues in other languages, consider asking your teacher to correct them.

When learning a new language, students are likely to make the following kinds of mistakes:

Misspelling: Because the sound a letter represents is language-dependent, spelling can be challenging. When in doubt, look the word up in your dictionary or textbook glossary.

Wrong word: A single word can have several distinct and unrelated meanings. The entire gist of a sentence can change if you translate the wrong definition. For example, consider how the exclamation "Duck!" could be translated as either a verb or a noun, with different results.

Incorrect tense or gender: Determining which verb form, article, or pronoun to use in a sentence can be complicated and confusing. Pay attention to your supplemental readings and the examples in your textbook to help understand these concepts. As you are reading, ask yourself why one tense or gender was chosen over another.

Faulty sentence structure: Languages differ in the how verbs, subjects, modifiers, and conjunctions are placed in a sentence. Even a simple sentence may be grammatically incorrect if translated word for word directly from English. The longer you study a language, the more experience you will gain in recognizing correct sentence constructions.

Misuse of an idiom: An idiom is an expression that has a meaning beyond the literal definition of the words. For example, the phrase "happy as a clam" does not mean that a person is no more or less joyful than the average mussel. Phrases such as "the last straw," "in the dog house," and "thick as thieves" might not make sense to someone who is not a native English speaker. Using idioms in another language can be tricky. It is easy to use an expression that is not suitable to the situation.

Students who learn a new language will make errors. Mistakes are an important part of the learning process. Try not to see errors as a sign that you are not talented at languages or unable to grasp a concept. Mistakes just mean you are stretching your skills. They show you are reaching out of your comfort zone with a language. See each mistake as a chance to improve your linguistic skills.

Tip 63: Pursue a goal.

The right goal can help you stay motivated to study a foreign language. An objective like one of the following can encourage you to practice verb conjugations:

- Take a summer or graduation trip to a country where they speak the language.

- Read a famous piece of literature in its original form.

- Participate in a school exchange program.

- Earn college credit or advanced standing.

- Talk with neighbors or family members in their native language.

- Watch a favorite foreign film without relying on the subtitles.

After you have selected a goal, write it down or cut out pictures that remind you of what you are looking forward to. Paste your reminder in your notebook, tuck it into your textbook, or tape it on a wall by your desk. When you are struggling with a vocabulary list or difficult grammatical concept, thinking about why you are learning the language can encourage you to keep working.

MATHEMATICS STUDY TIPS

For some students, mathematics can be the most challenge class on their schedule. Business, science, engineering, art, and music all rely on mathematical principles. With so many real world applications, it is just as important as ever to understand the material covered in your algebra, trigonometry, business math, and calculus classes.

WHY STUDY MATHEMATICS?

Students take mathematics for a variety of reasons. Many high schools have a minimum level of proficiency that must be achieved or a number of math classes that must be completed before a student can graduate. Some students take additional classes to prepare for the math sections of the ACT or SAT. Colleges may require students to achieve a certain level of mathematics mastery before they are admitted to the school or to some majors.

High schools and colleges emphasize mathematics as a core subject because it is an integral part of so many other areas of study. Engineers use mathematics to calculate the forces on the structures they design. Nurses and other healthcare professionals must figure out dilutions and dosages of medications. Scientists use equations to model the systems they study. For centuries, artists have recognized the importance of the "golden ratio" in creating balanced compositions. Music is also grounded in mathematics, with note values and tones built around fractions and multiples.

You are likely to encounter the mathematics concepts you learn in high school throughout your life. If you want to take out a loan for a house or car, understanding simple and compound interest will allow you to determine a payment plan that will fit your budget. If you are planning a garden or home improvement project, being able to accurately calculate the amount of material you need may save money.

Studying mathematics can also help develop logic and problem solving skills. The ability to take a list of data and use it to extrapolate new information is important in many professional fields, including the following.

Law: Detectives use what they know about crimes to direct investigations. Lawyers build cases using evidence.

Medicine: Physicians make diagnoses based on patients' symptoms. Nurses determine the best way to complete treatment plans based on patients' needs.

Graphic design: Graphic artists use design principles and clients' requirements to create logos, print advertisements, signs, and other forms of visual communication.

Management: Whether managing construction projects or a retail store, managers are expected to create schedules and budgets within a set of given restraints.

Computer science: Programmers put mathematical algorithms together to create software applications.

Some concepts you learn in math class can be used to streamline your daily activities. For example, a working knowledge of Boolean logic can make finding information on the Internet quicker and easier. Understanding fractions allows you to translate a recipe that makes four servings into one that will feed 10. A grasp on statistics will help you determine which service station gives you the best gas mileage at the lowest cost.

COMMON PROBLEMS

Mathematic concepts can be divided into two broad categories: theoretical and applied. Theoretical mathematics is the study of techniques used to manipulate numbers and variables. Applied mathematics is the process of using these techniques to solve problems.

Math classes cover both theoretical and applied principles. Students may have trouble understanding the theory of what they are learning. They may have trouble internalizing a concept unless they are given concrete examples. Examples of theory-related problems include:

- Not understanding the difference in a function and an equation

- Not understanding the relationship between integrals and geometric area

- Not understanding the connection between the solution of a two variable, two equation system and the graphs of those equations

- Not understanding how to solve an equation for an unknown

- Not understanding how to apply arithmetic operations to variables

Students who understand the theory may find it more challenging to solve applied problems. They may find themselves using equations correctly, but making errors in the addition, subtraction, multiplication, and need to practice basic arithmetic skills. Some common application problems include:

- Not reducing fractions correctly

- Miscalculating an integral

- Making errors when solving a system of equations

- Being able to reduce a fraction when it only contains variables, but having trouble reducing a numerical fraction or a fraction with both numbers and variables

Some students may find that crossing the bridge between theoretical and applied processes is difficult. These students may understand the concepts they learn about in class and be able to find the solution when given an equation, but they have trouble figuring out which process or function to use to solve a word problem. When students have trouble transferring their theoretical knowledge to a problem they may:

- Be unable to construct a system of equations based on information in a word problem, but have no trouble solving the system if it is given to them.

- Understand the concept of a mathematic average and be able to calculate the average of a set of numbers, but not feel confident about calculating their own grade in a class or their grade point average.

- Understand areas and be able to calculate the areas of geometric shapes, but feel overwhelmed if asked to determine how much carpet they will need for a room.

If you have trouble in math class, try to diagnose if your problems are related to understanding the theory you are learning, applying the theory, or making the jump from the theoretical to the applied. The following table gives some suggestions for ways to improve your comprehension of theoretical concepts, your ability to apply those concepts, and your understanding of the connection between theory and applications.

Suggestions for Solving Common Problems in Math Class		
Theory Comprehension Problems	**Application Problems**	**Connecting Theory to Application Problems**
Look up concepts in other textbooks or on the Internet for different explanations. Sometimes, a slightly different presentation of the same material can help a student understand a difficult idea. During class, ask for concrete examples of the concept you are studying. Later, try to recreate the abstract concept based on the example. Review previous sections of your notes and textbook. Mathematics is a cumulative subject. If you missed or forgot earlier information, you may not have the building blocks needed to comprehend the current material.	Drill on basic arithmetic and algebraic problems. Redo previous homework assignments, paying close attention to the steps used to solve the problems. Before turning in an assignment or test, check all your work. Show all your work when solving a problem. This will help you find errors and aid your teacher in diagnosing comprehension problems.	Ask your teacher to label what was done in each step on an example problem. Read through example problems in your textbook. Close the book and try to solve the problem. Refer back to the book if you become stuck. Practice applying the concepts you learn in class to life outside school (see Tip 70). Use flow charts to summarize problem solving processes.

Tip 64: Release your preconceptions.

Maybe you had trouble with a previous math class or scored low on a standardized test. Perhaps a parent, teacher, or classmate commented that you seemed to lack the mathematics gene. No matter how it happened, if your confidence in your mathematical ability is shattered, you may find it hard to succeed in class. If you are convinced you are not good at math, you are never going to be good at it.

Some students have a mental image of the type of person who is a good math student. Perhaps they think that one gender has more innate mathematical ability, that athletes cannot excel at math, or that some nations produce better math students than others. If you do not fit your own preconception of what a good math student is like, consider some people who made significant contributions to the subject:

- Theano (6th century BC): Greek mathematician, philosopher, teacher, and mother

- Emilie du Châtelet (1706-1749): French noblewoman, socialite, author, and mathematician

- Charlotte Angas Scott (1858-1931): First British woman to earn a PhD in mathematics, co-editor of the American Journal of Mathematics, and first woman accepted into the American Mathematical Society

- Sophie Piccard (1904-1990): Russian mathematician and founder of the Center for Pure Mathematics

- Herbert Earle Buchanan (1881-1974): College football player and coach, mathematics professor, vice president of the National Collegiate Athletic Association (NCAA), and founder of the Mathematics Association of America

- Euphemia Lofton Haynes (1890-1980): First African-American woman to earn a PhD in Mathematics, education activist, first vice-president of the Archdiocesan Council of Catholic Women, recipient of the Papal Medal

❧   Elbert F. Cox (1895-1969): First African-American to be awarded a PhD in mathematics, chair of mathematics and physics department at West Virginia State College and mathematics department at Howard University

❧   Richard Tapia (1939-): Mexican-American mathematician, recipient of the Presidential Award of Excellence in Science, Mathematics, and Engineering Mentoring, recipient of the Prize for Distinguished Service to the Profession by the Society for Industrial and Applied Mathematics

❧   Genevieve Madeline Knight (1939-): African-American mathematics professor and 1993 winner of the Mathematics Association of America Distinguished Teaching Award

There is no mold for mathematicians. Being good at math is not dependent on what you look like or what activities you participate in. Hard work, diligent practice, and focused study can help you succeed. If your preconceptions are holding you back, review the tips in Chapter 7 for help conquering the internal preconceptions that may be keeping you from achieving to your highest potential in math classes.

Tip 65: Realize that homework is not punishment.

For the most part, teachers do not assign mathematics homework to irritate you, ruin your weekend, or bore you. Mathematics is a skill-based subject. A homework assignment that seems tedious and repetitive to you may be designed to help you practice skills and master difficult concepts. Homework also gives your teacher a chance to identify areas that you do not seem to understand so they can be covered more thoroughly in class.

As you practice your math skills, you are also developing your own problem solving style. The experience you gain in evaluating a problem and forming a plan of attack will come in handy on class exams and standardized tests. The more assignments you complete, the more opportunities you have to see what approaches work best for you.

If you find it difficult to concentrate on math long enough to complete your homework assignment, break your study session into several short segments. Sandwich your math work with tasks that require less focus. Review the tips in Chapter 1 for more ways to organize your study session to work as efficiently as possible.

Tip 66: Show all your work on every problem.

You might think it is obvious how you got from step A to step B, but your teacher might not understand your reasoning, especially if you made an arithmetic or logical error. On an exam or graded assignment, leaving out steps can lower your chances of getting partial credit for a problem.

Try to show all your work on problems you work in your notes, too. A process that is clear to you while you are writing your notes may seem confusing later when you are trying to study. Having all the steps you used to arrive at a solution can help you work through the problem again.

When showing your work for a problem, take into account the following guidelines:

- Write out all the information given in the problem.

- State what you are trying to solve for.

- ❦ Define any variables you use.

- ❦ Show all reduced or expanded equations.

- ❦ Work neatly in a single column down your paper.

- ❦ Write and label any standard formulas and equations before you use them in your calculations.

- ❦ Make sure that the progression between every step is clear.

- ❦ Circle your final answer.

Tip 67: Do your own work.

If you are stuck on a difficult problem or do not have time to complete an assignment, you may be tempted to turn to the Internet or to a friend for help.

Depending on the rules set for the class, school, and assignment, looking at examples from books and Web sites or listening while classmates explain their problem solving process may be acceptable. However, copying an answer exactly from any source is academic plagiarism.

If you are stuck and feel you need to look at how someone solved a similar problem, put the example away before you work on yours. That way, you can be certain that the work you turn in is your own.

When stuck on a difficult problem on a homework assignment, these suggestions might help:

- Look up any terms or equations in the problem.

- Review your notes and textbook. Try to find an example similar to the challenging problem. Work through the example, then try to solve the assigned problem again.

- Avoid using a search engine to find the exact problem.

- Ask a friend or family member to solve a problem similar to the assigned problem. Ask questions about any steps you do not understand. After you understand how they solved the sample problem, try to solve the assigned problem by yourself.

- Work through the assigned problem as far as you can, then ask a friend of family member about the specific step you are having trouble with.

- After completing the challenging problem, review your work to make sure you understand the solution. Reinforce what you learned by solving a similar problem.

Tip 68: Read your book.

If you only refer to your math textbook to copy assigned problems, you may be missing out on some examples, explanations, and diagrams that could help you understand the theoretical and applied concepts you are learning in class.

If you never flip past the problem sections in your textbook, you may be missing features like:

- Lists of steps involved in solving types of problems

- Different forms of equations

- Annotated examples

- Connections in applications and theoretical concepts

- Reviews of definitions and functions covered earlier in the semester or in previous classes

- Profiles of careers that use math

Study your mathematics book using the same critical reading techniques you would employ to learn history, science, or language arts. For more information about getting the most out of your textbook, review the tips in Chapter 5.

Tip 69: Do not rely on a calculator.

Modern calculators can graph equations, reduce fractions, solve for variables, determine derivatives, find integrals, and calculate trigonometric values. Powerful and versatile calculators can become a crutch for students who do not understand the principles they are using. As long students know the right buttons to push, they can solve certain problems. However, if they are given the information in a slightly different form they may become lost.

Do not allow yourself to become dependent on a calculator. Make sure you understand how to solve problems by hand. Ask your teacher to work out examples on the board so that you can see how variables and constants are being used. If you do not understand the connection between the buttons you are pressing and the numbers you see on the calculator's screen, make sure you ask for clarification.

You may be able to earn a good grade in a math class by learning to memorizing which calculator buttons to press, but that does not guarantee that you have gained a firm grasp of the principles that will lay a foundation for your future studies.

Tip 70: Seek out ways to practice math skills in real life.

Look for ways to practice your skills outside math class. The practice will help hone your skills, and it will reinforce the importance of mathematics in every day situations. Some ways to apply mathematics to your daily activities include:

- Keep a running total of your shopping costs.

- Design an art or craft project based on a geometric shape or transcendental number.

- Chart your gas mileage for gas purchased at different filling stations.

- Calculate your change when you make a purchase with cash.

- Figure out how much money you are earning at your summer or after school job.

- Determine the average speed maintained when you travel to school.

Practice can help you improve your speed, accuracy, and understanding of math skills. By making mathematics a larger part of your life, you can also develop your confidence with and enjoyment of the subject.

Language Arts
Study Tips

"Language arts" is an umbrella term for a range of subjects that focus on oral or written communication. Classes that may be grouped in your school's language arts department include:

- **English:** English classes cover grammar rules, vocabulary, literature, and composition.

- **Communications:** Communications curricula include media studies, journalism, and public speaking.

- **Drama:** In drama classes, students read, study, and perform plays.

Why Study Language Arts?

The ability to communicate is integral to many academic subjects, after school activities, and vocations. Home contractors need to be able to talk with clients to understand what they want and to explain problems. Science students may have to prepare laboratory reports. Retailers should be able to explain the benefits of their products to potential customers. History students may need to answer essay questions on examinations. Effective teachers must be able to explain material in ways that their students can understand.

Language arts classes can help develop reading comprehension skills. The ability to understand written material can help you study other subjects more efficiently. Studying literature can also help develop critical thinking proficiency. Mastering grammar rules and common writing styles can help you develop well written essays, reports, and stories in any subject.

COMMON PROBLEMS

Students in language arts classes may have trouble with reading comprehension, writing ability, or oral communication. Signs of a reading comprehension problem include:

- Trouble reading material fluently

- Difficulty understanding certain words

- Misidentifying the main idea of a passage

- Difficulty finding details in a passage

- Rereading a section several times to understand it

Students who have trouble writing effectively may:

- Be unaware of basic grammar rules

- Have trouble identifying grammatical errors

> Lack a large working vocabulary

> Find it difficult to group supporting ideas with a main idea to compose a paragraph

Some common oral communication problems include:

> Experiencing extreme nervousness when asked to speak in public

> Veering off topic during an extemporaneous speech

> Difficulty following an outline or notes when giving a speech

Effective oral and written communication skills are important both in school and after graduation, but they do not come easily for many students. The tips in this chapter can help you succeed in your language arts classes.

Tip 71: Keep up with readings.

Language arts classes often include large amounts of reading. In English class, you may need to read novels, short stories, textbook chapters, and essays. Drama students may be assigned plays or scripts. In communication classes, you may be responsible for articles and transcripts.

If you put off your assigned readings, you may find yourself in a situation where you have to read several essays in a night or a large novel over a weekend. Even if you are a fast reader, compressing your reading load into a short time can result in many problems. Possible problems that can occur from putting off assigned readings include the following:

Reduced comprehension: It can be difficult to understand material that you read when you are fatigued.

Less enjoyment: If you are watching the clock and trying to read faster to catch up on your assignments, you may not enjoy the story, essay, or novel as much as you would have if you read it at a more leisurely pace.

Less time to work on related assignments: Your struggle to finish reading a novel may eat into the time you scheduled to work on the associated report.

Do not let yourself fall behind on your readings. Divide large assignments into manageable chunks using the techniques described in Chapter 6. Depending on the type of material you are reading, you may find it useful to divide the assignment based on:

- Page
- Chapter
- Stanza
- Paragraph
- Scene
- Act
- Heading or subheading

Tackling assigned readings a little at a time rather than trying to read it all at once will help you avoid become overly tired or bored with the assignment.

Tip 72: Go beyond skimming.

Skimming is a useful technique when reading a textbook or article just to find a definition, equation, or date, but when studying for a language arts class you may need to read material more closely.

When you are reading a play, short story, or novel, you need to look beyond the surface details of the material. Use the following questions to help guide your reading:

- From what point of view is the story told?

- Why did the author choose those words?

- What motivates the character's behavior?

- Why do you feel sympathetic toward a particular character?

- Why did the author choose that setting?

- Are there any repeated images in the piece?

- What symbols are used?

- What are the relationships between the characters?

- How have the characters changed by the end?

Ask yourself the questions you think are likely to show up on an exam. Keep a list of questions you are unable to answer so that you can bring them up during class discussions.

Tip 73: Invest in a good reference book.

There are many rules and conventions people use when communicating through writing. Using correct grammar may seem boring, outdated, and unimportant, but when you break the rules of writing, you may face some consequences, including the following:

Ambiguous meaning: Poor punctuation, sentence structure, or word choices can confuse your reader.

Inappropriate tone: Readers expect a certain level of formality from academic writing. If you write in dialect, they may question your logic or education.

Lower grade: Because one of the objective of studying language arts is to polish your written communication skills, your teacher may take off points for grammatical errors.

A grammar guide is useful when you have questions about where to place a comma or what pronoun to use. There are several English reference books on the market, including:

- *The Little Brown Essential Handbook* by Jane E. Aaron

- *The Elements of Style* by William Strunk, Jr. and E.B. White

- *The Blue Book of Grammar and Punctuation* by Jane Straus

- *Checking Your Grammar: Scholastic Guides* by Marvin Terban

Look for a guide that you find easy-to-use and understand. A good grammar book can be useful through high school, college, and your professional life, so opt for one with a durable binding.

Tip 74: Know what your teacher wants.

Even a well-researched, highly structured, innovative, and thoughtful essay may earn a lackluster grade if it is not on the topic assigned by the teacher.

The first step in writing a successful paper or answering an essay question is deciphering what your teacher wants. Some common terms used in topics for language arts writing assignments include "analyze," "compare," "contrast," "define," and "discuss."

ANALYZE

The term "analyze" means to divide the subject into small parts. Writing an analysis involves listing the subject's components. When composing an analysis, you may find the following transitional phrases useful:

- "The first..."
- "The next..."
- "The last..."
- "Another..."
- "An additional..."
- "The main..."
- "Subsequent..."
- "In addition..."
- "As a result..."
- "Because of this..."

Example: Analyze the ramifications of the entailment on the Bennet family's estate in *Pride and Prejudice*.

As a result of the entailment, Mr. and Mrs. Bennet needed to have a son to keep the estate from passing to a distant cousin when Mr. Bennet died. In the hopes of having a boy, they produced more children than they could afford on the family's income. With no money set aside to ensure the welfare of their five daughters, the Bennets' only hope became to marry at least one daughter into a wealthy family. An additional consequence of the entailment is the connection of the Bennets to Mr. Collins. As the heir to the Bennet estate, Mr. Collins must be welcomed into Longbourne and accepted into the Bennets' social circle.

COMPARE

To compare two subjects means to detail the similarities between the two. Some of the phrases you may use to help a comparison flow include:

- "Similarly..."
- "In the same way..."
- "In a similar manner..."
- "Likewise..."
- "Correspondingly"

> **Example: Compare the personalities of Jake Barnes and Brett Ashley in *The Sun Also Rises*.**
>
> Jake and Brett are similar in their self-destructive behavior and their outlooks on life. In the same way that Jake's drinking keeps him in a job that he does not enjoy, Brett's continuous jumping from one relationship to another keeps her from dealing with her personal insecurities.
>
> Both Jake and Brett picture better lives for themselves that would have been possible except for the war and Jake's injury. They are both unable to move on because they cannot give up the fantasy of what life could have been like. Like the rest of the Lost Generation (as characterized by the book), they blame all the disappointment in their lives on the war.

CONTRAST

When you are asked to contrast two objects, you should analyze the differences between them. The following terms indicate that you are contrasting two people, events, places, or situations:

- "On the other hand..."
- "However..."
- "Conversely..."
- "As a contrast to..."

Example: Contrast the life experiences of Howard Roark and Dominique Francon in *The Fountainhead*.

The life experiences of Roark and Francon diverge at an early age. While Francon grew up in a life of privilege, educated in private schools and vacationing in luxury, Roark was orphaned as a boy and supported himself by working odd jobs in the construction industry.

As a contrast to Roark's solitary existence in school, Francon was a budding socialite. According to her father, she was always surrounded by a mob of schoolmates although she never had a close friend. That popularity continued into her adult years, even when she held her admirers in open disdain.

Roark chose his professional field, architecture, when he was young and approaches his work with intensity. Francon, on the other hand, treats her popular newspaper column as a hobby. She does not know what she wants to do with her life and is only marking time with her job.

DEFINE

To define a term means to identify the larger group or groups the term belongs to and analyze the attributes that distinguish the term from other members of the group or groups. Begin a definition by stating the term you will be defining. The following examples show different formats that can be used to categorize and then differentiate a term.

Define "novella."

> A novella is a written piece of fictional prose that has more than 17,500 words and less than 40,000 words.

Define "assonance."

> Assonance is a literary device in which an internal vowel sound is repeated.

Define Holden Caulfield's role in his family in *The Catcher in the Rye*.

Holden is the second oldest child in a family of three boys and one girl. Unlike the other siblings, Holden plays the role of the protector. He hides the fact that his mother bought the wrong kind of ice skates because he does not want to hurt her feelings. He obsesses over his little sister's emotional well-being and his older brother's career choices. Holden blames himself for his younger brother's death, even though he cognitively realizes he was not at fault.

DISCUSS

In language arts assignments, to discuss means to analyze and then expound upon the subject's component parts. A discussion may include definitions, opinions, comparisons, and contrasts.

Example: Discuss the elements of fiction.

The elements of fiction include the characters, plot, setting, and theme of the story in addition to the author's style. The five elements of style work together to unify the piece.

The characters are the personalities involved in the story. Their decisions, experiences, and thoughts dictate the plot, or the set of actions, of the piece. The setting of the story is the time and location where the actions take place. Characters' actions can be influenced by the setting. The theme of the story overarching message of the piece as revealed through the plot.

The style is the mechanics of the writing. Style includes the words, sentence structures, literary devices, and format the author uses to develop the characters, describe the setting, create the plot, and reveal the theme of the piece.

These examples would be appropriate responses to a short answer section of an exam. If you were writing a paper on one of the given topics, you would need to explore each idea you mention more fully by defining terms and providing multiple examples for your assertions.

Tip 75: Let it rest.

Plan to put your essays away for a day so you can proofread them with fresh eyes. Taking time away from your paper will allow you to detach your emotions from the work. When you can look at your writing dispassionately, you are more likely to notice grammar errors, structural issues, and logic flaws.

You may not always have time to put an assignment away for a day before giving it a final reading and polish. Your teacher may give you only one day to work on smaller papers, the assignment may have taken longer than you expected to complete, or you may have waited until the last minute to start. If time is short, delaying the final proofread for even an hour can be beneficial.

Letting your papers rest before you produce the final draft will allow you to look at your paper with fresh eyes and help you turn in the best work you can produce.

Tip 76: Veer off the reading list.

Keeping up with your language arts class may require you to read material that you would not choose for yourself or do not find interesting. You may get more out of the concepts you are learning at school by reading other works by authors you are reading in class, books from the same time period, or articles about the same topic. Reading material related to the works you are studying in class can help you understand the themes of your assigned readings and write more nuanced essays.

Even reading material completely unrelated to your language arts assignments can improve your oral and written communication proficiency by helping you:

- Develop a larger working vocabulary.

- Practice reading for content.

- Increase reading speed.

- Gain exposure to different writing styles.

- Learn about other people, times, and ideas.

When you read books, articles, or short stories connected to the material you are studying in your language arts class, you may enjoy additional benefits such as:

Recognizing the importance of setting in character, plot, and theme development: By reading narratives that take place in the same area or time period, you can gain a better understanding of the defining elements of that setting.

Becoming more familiar with the style of a writer: When you read several books, stories, poems, or plays by the same writer, you will be better prepared to identify which literary devices are characteristic of the author's style and which ones are used only rarely to achieve a particular effect.

Increased familiarity with literary forms: For example, reading a variety of poetry will help you become more aware of the differences between sonnets, ballads, and haikus.

You may want to choose supplemental readings based on the following criteria:

Author: When studying a novel or play in a language arts class, consider reading other compositions written by the same author.

This will help you develop a better feel for the author's writing style, and it will give you a chance to identify themes or character traits that may be repeated in several works.

Theme: Poetry and fictional prose often address basic aspects of the human condition, including love, hate, jealousy, fear, guilt, and compassion. If you are assigned a novel or short story with a theme that you find intriguing, seek out other pieces that deal with a similar idea. Reading more about the idea can lead to a deeper understanding of the literary theme.

Date written: Authors can be influenced by the local and global events occurring as they write. Exploring other works written around the same time as an assigned reading can help you understand the historical framework.

Setting: Reading multiple works set in the same time and location can help you understand different perspectives of the same events.

Author's nationality: Reading pieces from several writers who identify with a single nationality can help you learn about the traditions, prejudices, and common experiences of other cultures.

Make time in your daily schedule to read supplemental material in addition to completing your required reading. The reading practice helps develop comprehension skills that are crucial for academic and professional success, and it helps you develop a deeper understanding of and appreciation for the literature you study in your language arts class.

Case Study: Julia D. Brown

Julia D. Brown

High School Teacher

I have a study skills activity that works well with small collaborative groups in language arts, science, or social studies classes. It is called "Tear It Up!" It uses a multi-chaptered paperback novel in language arts or copies of a chapter with divisions in science or social studies that pertains to the subject or author we are studying.

The novel or chapter is torn apart by chapter or subdivision and given to the students, who are assigned to read and annotate their sections. They are also required to come up with one or two questions about their sections.

As a group, the students come together and share their chapters or sections and questions. In a short time, a complete novel or textbook assignment can be read and studied.

HISTORY STUDY TIPS

History is the study of the causes and effects of events in the past. High school history courses may cover actions that occurred thousands of years ago through events of recent decades. Students may be required to memorize dates, names, and locations associated with important incidents. They may also be responsible for understanding the tactics, motivations, strengths, and weaknesses of historical figures.

WHY STUDY HISTORY?

You may need to pass one or more history classes to graduate from high school. Common required classes include western civilization and American history. In addition, you may be required to complete a course about the history of a particular state or ethnicity.

Knowledge of history can help you in many other subjects. If you are interested in current events and politics, familiarity with the conflicts and social situations of the past can help you understand the root causes of contemporary conditions. You may be able to understand and enjoy literature, music, and art more by studying the historical circumstances under which they were created. Learning about the history of a people or an area can help you develop a more well-rounded approach toward anthropology and sociology.

Common Problems

Students may find history a difficult subject to learn for a variety of reasons. Some students may enjoy understand the concepts they read about, but have trouble memorizing data. Others may find it hard to see the cause and effect relationships between historical events. It is common for high school students to see history as nothing more than a list of facts that hold little importance to their lives.

Far from being irrelevant, history is at the core of how people dress, speak, think, and work. Studying history can be challenging, but the reward is a better understanding of your world, your society, and yourself.

Tip 77: Put facts in context.

An important tenant in the study of history is that nothing happens in a vacuum. This means that there are always causal and parallel activities. Causal activities are actions that lead directly to an event. Parallel activities happened at the same time as the event, but were not directly related. For example, the secession of the South from the United States in 1861 was a causal event leading to the American Civil War. During the same year, the Kingdom of Italy was established, Benito Juárez was elected President of Mexico, and the Taiping Rebellion continued. These events happened in parallel to the American Civil War as they were not directly connected.

Unfortunately, there may not be enough class time for your teacher to cover all the causes of an important historical event or the parallel activities that happened at the same time. This can give the impression that history is a series of disjointed events occurring at irregular intervals during which nothing happened. For many students, this list of facts can be boring to study and difficult to memorize.

If you have trouble remembering when events happened, look outside the vacuum. Find out what happened to cause the events, and what was going on in the rest of the world at the same time. Try to relate the history you need to learn for class to the history that interests you. If you enjoy music, research what styles were popular during that time and what compositions were being created. If you enjoy literature, find out what writers were producing at the time.

Visual tools such as timelines and maps can help you understand the context of the material you are studying in class. Timelines arrange events in chronological order. You can create a timeline that shows only the causes and effects of an event or one that also includes parallel activities. A national, state, regional, or world map can be labeled to show events that occurred in different geographic locations over the course of a specific time.

Think about how parallel activities may have influenced the people you are learning about. For example, Abraham Lincoln may have listened to compositions by Franz Liszt and read a Victor Hugo novel during his presidency. Seeing the broader picture of history instead of the narrow window presented by many textbooks can make the subject more fun to study and more relevant to your personal experiences.

Tip 78: Create and use flashcards.

Flashcards are pieces of paper with a term, phrase, or question on one side, and related information on the opposite side. Flashcards can help tactile, auditory, and visual learners memorize important dates, names, locations, and other facts for history classes.

Flashcards can be as simple or as fancy as you like. Standard index cards make good flashcard blanks because they are sturdy, easy to hold, inexpensive, and readily available in a variety of colors. However, you can make flashcards out of other materials, such as:

- Notebook or copier paper

- Poster board

- Envelopes

- Manila folders

Tactile learners can benefit from holding and turning each card to read the front and the back. Auditory learners may learn more efficiently by reading the cards aloud or having someone use the cards as props in an oral quiz. Visual learners may find it helpful to see the information on each side of the card.

The process of researching and creating flashcards can help you become more familiar with the material. Each time you read the flashcards or use them to quiz yourself, you will be improving your ability to recall the information during tests or class discussions.

Case Study: Justin Pawlicki

Justin Pawlicki

College Resident Assistant

Index cards are good study aids. Write a fact on each one, wrap a rubber band around the deck, and keep them in your backpack to flip through whenever you have time.

Tip 79: Understand your teacher's perspective.

History classes can be hotbeds for disagreements because the causes and effects of events are often open to interpretation. Even if your opinion differs from your teacher's, you may believe that you need to answer test questions or complete homework assignments from your teacher's viewpoint to get a good grade.

Teachers should not penalize you for having different opinions about an event, but you do need to understand your teacher's perspective so that you can defend your own. Each generation tends to look at history in a different way. An important step in appreciating your teachers' positions is to learn about the events and social conditions that helped shape their life experiences. The following table describes common pivotal events for people born in different decades.

Formative Experiences for Different Generations	
Birth Year	**Notes**
Before 1946	Because members of the "Builder generation" lived through World War II, they tend to be patriotic and politically conservative. They may have grown up in families still recovering from the Great Depression and developed frugal habits. Respect for elders and people in positions of authority was stressed when the Builders were growing up, and they may expect a higher level of formality than other

Formative Experiences for Different Generations	
Birth Year	**Notes**
	teachers. Builders lived through some of the most fascinating events of modern history and are uniquely positioned to give their students first-hand accounts.
1946-1964	Baby Boomers tend to be less frugal than Builders. This was the first generation that made substantial purchases on credit. More Baby Boomers went to college than previous generations. As a group, they are more open-minded than their predecessors.
1964-1980	Unlike Builders and Baby Boomers, members of Generation X were likely to grow up in a family where both parents worked. They tend to be more independent and open-minded than previous generations. They may expect students to be self-motivated learners and to complete assignments with little instruction or structure. Most are comfortable with technology.
1980-1994	As children, more Generation Y members grew up in dual-income homes than previous generations. A percentage also grew up in blended families. Many members of Generation Y were encouraged to question authority. They grew up in a society immersed in computers and tend to be comfortable using high-tech tools.

It is impossible to pigeonhole teachers based on their age, but understanding the trends for different generations may help you understand the basis for a teacher's behavior and pinpoint reasons for problems. Age is not the only factor that shapes people's perspectives. Religious beliefs, socioeconomic situation, and personal experiences are also important factors.

If you feel that a teacher is discriminating against you because of your views, there are different options for you to take, including the following.

Save any papers that you believe you received a lower grade on than you deserved because you stated an opinion different than the teacher's. If your teacher wants to keep your assignments, ask if you can make copies.

Talk to your teacher about your concerns. Bring graded assignments and tests that you think show your teacher's bias. Try to be open-minded when discussing the issue. It may turn out that you lost points on homework or exams because you stated historical inaccuracies, failed to answer the question, or used faulty logic, not because of your views.

Talk to an adult. A trusted parent, coach, or teacher should know about the situation in case the biasness continues.

You should not have to compromise your values or beliefs to earn a good grade in a history class. Teachers that use the classroom to espouse political agendas or demand you support a particular religious creed may be creating an uncomfortable environment and derailing your ability to learn.

Tip 80: Seek out other resources.

Your teacher and textbooks should not be your only sources when learning history. First-hand accounts, historical fiction, mainstream nonfiction, and documentaries can help you understand key ideas, become familiar with other perspectives, and remember facts.

Unfortunately, not all resources provide accurate and complete information. In particular, written historical fiction and movies based on facts tend to change, exaggerate, or downplay facts for the benefit of the plotline.

Before trusting the information in a book, television show, or movie to help you on your next history test, consider the following questions:

Who wrote the book or script? Find out who created the resource.

What are their qualifications? Does the writer have an academic background in history or have they lived through the events documented in the resource?

Does the publisher, writer, or director have an agenda? The resource may have been produced to promote a particular viewpoint.

Does the resource claim to be fiction or nonfiction? Works of historical fiction can give you a better feel for life in a different time or place and may help you understand the relationships between people and events, but they may not be accurate.

What grade level was the resource created for? A movie or book produced for younger students may present a watered-down version of events.

Your librarian or history teacher may be able to recommend written or visual media to supplement your textbook and class discussions.

Tip 81: Create a narrative.

History is a web of linked events, with characters, climaxes, and surprises. One way to help remember the facts about a historic event and understand how incidents are connected is to create a story including the causes and effects you are studying.

Creating a narrative can help make the material seem less dry and more interesting. The process can also help you prepare for exams. As you study, tell yourself the historical story. Repeat it to your study partners and family members. The more you repeat your narrative the easier you will find it to recall the material during the test.

Tip 82: Make cause and effect puzzles.

Cause and effect puzzles are a way of testing and reinforcing your understanding of the relationships between historical events. To create a puzzle, make a list of causes and effects related to the era you are studying. For example, you might make the following list about World War I:

Causes and Effects of World War I	
Causes	**Effects**
Archduke Ferdinand and wife are assassinated by the Serbian "Black Hand" nationalist group.	Austria-Hungary sent a strongly worded demand for the assassins to be turned over. The demand is so strong it questions Serbia's sovereignty.
Austria-Hungary demanded the assassins' extradition.	Serbia exercised its historic ties to Russia to bring about a defense agreement.
Serbia-Russia formed a defense agreement.	Austria-Hungary sought a similar arrangement with Germany, whose Keiser was looking to expand Germany's influence.
Serbian denied the Austria-Hungarian extradition demand.	Austria-Hungary declared war on Serbia.
Austria-Hungary declared war on Serbia.	Russia began mobilizing a defense army toward Serbia.
Russian mobilization efforts were seen as a threat to Austria-Hungary by Germany.	Germany declared war on Russia.
France had an existing military treaty with Russia.	Germany declared war on France.

Causes and Effects of World War I	
Causes	**Effects**
Germany invaded neutral Belgium as a way of shortening the distance to Paris.	Britain, under a 75 year old defense pact, was obligated to defend Belgium. Britain declared war on Germany, and by extension, on Austria-Hungary. The rest of the British Empire, including Canada, Australia, South Africa, India, and New Zealand, followed.
Japan had treaty with Britain promising mutual support.	Japan declared war with Germany.
Japan declared war with Germany.	Germany and Austria-Hungary declared war with Japan.
German submarines sank the American ship Lusitania three years after the war began.	United States declared war on Germany/ Austria-Hungary.

Next, arrange the items on the list into a network, with the causes connected to the appropriate effects. If you want your cause and effect puzzle to be sturdy, draw the network on a piece of cardstock or pasteboard. Add any details you need to learn about each cause or effect. In the sample network that follows, the arrows show how some events caused others.

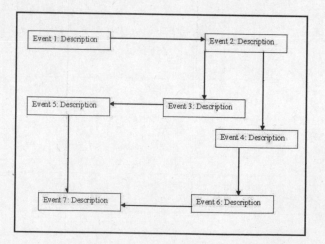

Finally, use scissors to cut the paper on which you drew the network into a series of freeform shapes. Cut the shapes so that each shape contains a single event, as in the following example.

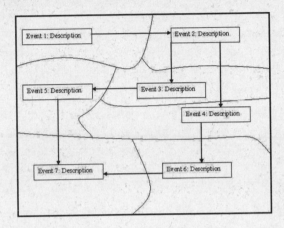

To study using the cause and effect puzzle, mix up the cut pieces and then reassemble the network. As you position each piece, read the description. Repeat the process as often as you can over the course of several days until you feel comfortable with the material on the network.

Resealable plastic bags are handy for keeping puzzle pieces organized. If you prepare more than one cause and effect puzzle, use a permanent market to write the name of the main event at the center of each network on the appropriate storage bag. For an additional challenge, mix up the pieces for two or more related puzzles and try to reassemble both networks.

Case Study: Catherine Engle

Catherine Engle

High School Teacher

As a student, I had to make lists and notecards to break down the important information from dry social studies texts. I use the same strategy in my classroom by using PowerPoint presentations that outline the material.

This is especially helpful with my special needs students and low level readers. I have taught my students to use PowerPoint and they have made study outlines this way for themselves. The screens do not intimidate them like a formal outline would. No cutting and pasting is allowed, but pictures to illustrate an event are okay. They can then use the notes for my essay tests.

We also use Post-Its to organize material. In study groups, they put the important information on Post-Its. They can then create lists or sequences with the sticky notes on a background paper. At first, the high school students did not buy into this, but they eventually created games with them and had some fun while learning.

Using a planner is a good idea. Actually, we have school agendas but the high school kids do not use them for planning much. Two of my best students, however, use them religiously.

SCIENCE

STUDY TIPS

Science is the study of natural laws and processes. High school science is often divided into several different courses, including:

- **Biology:** Biology is the science of the chemical and physical processes associated with living organisms. Biology classes may cover ecology, physiology, anatomy, and botany.

- **Geology:** Geology is the study of the current and past structure of the earth.

- **Chemistry:** Chemistry is the science of how elements, molecules, and compounds behave and interact.

- **Physics:** Physics is the study of how time, matter, and motion behave on earth and in space.

Other subjects such as computer science and psychology are sometimes included in a high school science department.

Why Study Science?

To study science is to better understand the physical and chemical forces that influence every part of daily life. How high you jump when grabbing a rebound at a basketball game is controlled by electrical and chemical reactions in your muscles and nerves. The ability of shampoo to clean your hair is the result of the molecular structure of the detergents and surfactants in the formula.

High school students are encouraged to study science because it helps them learn about the world around them, and because it helps them form a framework for learning that can be applied to other fields. This framework is called the scientific method.

The scientific method is a process of inquiry that includes questioning, researching, hypothesizing, experimenting, analyzing, and interpreting.

Questioning

The scientific method begins when a researcher forms a question. Scientific questions come in many forms, including:

- Why does this happen?

- What would happen if this were changed?

- By what process do these entities interact?

- What will be the result if this trend continues?

RESEARCHING

The first step in trying to answer a question using the scientific method is to become familiar with the topic through research. Research methods may include observing the subject, reading books and articles, and talking with experts. In the process of researching, investigators may realize that their questions have already been answered.

HYPOTHESIZING

Once investigators learn as much as possible about their questions, they use their knowledge to propose possible answers to the questions.

EXPERIMENTING

Next, investigators construct experiments to test their hypotheses. All reagents and results of experiments must be measured accurately so that the tests can be repeated if needed.

ANALYZING

After the experiments are completed, investigators must analyze the data. Analysis may include calculating statistical values that can be used when interpreting the results.

INTERPRETING

Once the raw data has been analyzed, investigators review the information and determine whether or not the results of the experiments support their hypotheses. They decide if additional experiments are needed to test the hypotheses. The scientific method is a cycle. Often the results of one experiment lead to more questions and the process begins again.

Use of the scientific method is not limited to biology, geology, chemistry, and physics research. The same process can be used in other fields, including the following:

Computer science: The scientific method can be used to pinpoint the cause of computer glitches and optimize algorithms.

Sports and exercise physiology: Athletes want their peak performance levels to correspond with important competitions. The scientific method can be used to determine how much an athlete should train and when is the peak time to taper.

Marketing: Analysts can use the scientific method to see how consumers respond to different advertising campaigns and calculate where and how marketing dollars would be most effectively spent.

Engineering: Engineers use the scientific method to streamline building processes and develop new materials.

Agriculture: The scientific method can help farmers determine the most cost-effective crops to plant in different fields.

The scientific method can be used in many nonacademic situations. It is useful to learn because it can be applied to many different areas in every day life. From determining which brand of food your cats prefer to optimizing your jump shot, the scientific method provides a strong framework for inquiry and discovery.

COMMON PROBLEMS

Some high school students find scientific concepts difficult to master. Some common problems include:

Difficulty memorizing: Students may have a hard time remembering definitions and processes. Science uses a specialized vocabulary. Students may need to look up terms and commit the definitions to memory to understand material. In addition, some words have different meanings in a science setting than in other situations. For example, in casual conversations, the word "theory" means an opinion or educated guess. When talking about science, a "theory" is the highest level of explanation for a large body of collected information.

Trouble drawing conclusions from results: The experiments performed or read about in high school science classes are designed to illustrate concepts. Students may be expected to interpret the results of the experiments and draw conclusions based on those results. They may need to extrapolate the information from the experiments to make broader predictions. Students may have problems making the jump from single examples to larger situations.

Visualization: Students may encounter scientific processes that are too small, such as molecular bonds, or too large, such as population dynamics, to examine first-hand. Some students may have trouble visualizing these processes based on written descriptions or simple drawings in their textbooks.

Disinterest: If students find the material they are studying in science class boring and dry, they may find it hard to pay attention in class or stay motivated to study at home.

Tip 83: Strive for understanding, not memorization.

When studying science, it is more efficient to focus on understanding concepts instead of only trying to memorize details and definitions. If you comprehend the process you are studying, you are more likely to be able to work out matching and short answer questions on a test even if they are about details you did not spend much time on. On the other hand, if you have simply learned a list of facts by rote, you may not be prepared to answer any questions except those related to the data committed to your memory.

Tip 84: Study diagrams.

When studying for science class, pay extra attention to the diagrams in your lecture notes and assigned textbook readings as they are often visual summaries of the reactions, cycles, and processes you are learning about.

When studying a diagram, make sure you can reproduce the information accurately and in the right order. If the diagram uses any terms you do not understand, look them up in your glossary or dictionary and write the definitions in your notes. Study the transition points and make sure you understand how the pieces of the diagram fit together.

After studying a diagram, close your textbook or notes and try to reproduce the drawing. Compare your diagram to the original copy in the textbook. Notice areas where you made errors or left out information. Continue to study the diagram, paying close attention to the areas where you made errors, until you can recreate it accurately and feel confident with the material.

Reproducing diagrams can be especially effective for visual learners. Tactile learners may benefit from creating puzzles based on science diagrams by using the described in Tip 82.

Tip 85: Create mnemonics to make memorization tasks easier.

In addition to understanding the concepts you learn about in science class, you may need to memorize definitions, lists, and processes. For example, it may not be sufficient to understand how to use the Ideal Gas Law. You may also need to memorize the corresponding equation to pass the exam.

Mnemonic devices are words, phrases, or sentences that help you remember information. Mnemonics are especially good for lists that you need to remember in order, for example the position of the planets in the solar system.

One way to create a mnemonic is to write a sentence based on the first letters of the terms in the ordered list you need to memorize. Each word in the mnemonic sentence should begin with the same letter as the term that is in the same position in the list.

For example, if you want to remember the steps of cellular mitosis, you could create a mnemonic sentence based on the following ordered list:

1. Interphase

2. Prophase

3. Metaphase

4.   Anaphase

5.   Telophase

6.   Cytokinesis

The mnemonic sentence needs to have words that begin with the following letters: I, P, M, A, T, C. Some examples of mnemonic sentences that could help students remember the order of the steps in cellular mitosis are:

❦   "I purchased my aunt the car."

❦   "Ida paid more alligators to cry."

❦   "If Paul made Mark telephone Casey."

❦   "I'll practice music after Ted cooks."

Notice that the sentence maintains the order from the list.

The same mnemonic technique can be applied to equations. Consider the following example using the Ideal Gas Law equation, $PV=nRT$:

❦   "Phillip's voice equals noise," roared Tori.

❦   Portia viewed equal notions regarding time.

❦   Patient visionaries equal nodding red tomatoes.

The most effective mnemonic tools tend to be:

❦   Easier to remember than the information they relate to

🐝 Vivid and descriptive

🐝 Simple

Mnemonic devices can help students memorize information, but they do not replace studying and understanding the material. A student who can explain mitosis but is unable to remember the terms for each phase may score better on a biology exam than a classmate who is able to recite the phases accurately but does not understand the process.

Tip 86: Realize the importance of laboratory experiments.

Laboratory experiences are important components of many high school science programs. Teachers may have many goals when scheduling labs. Laboratory units may be geared toward:

🐝 Offering students the chance to use equipment they may encounter in vocational training or college science classes.

🐝 Familiarizing students with the scientific method.

🐝 Disproving common or historic scientific misconceptions such as spontaneous generation or Lamarckian inheritance.

🐝 Demonstrating key concepts.

🐝 Reinforcing material covered in class lectures or textbook readings.

🐝 Maintaining or increasing student interest in the subject.

☙ Giving students a chance to burn off energy.

☙ Laboratory experiences may be especially important for tactile learners, as they offer a hands-on learning opportunity.

To help get the most out of a science lab, take a few minutes after class to review what you did. Write down the procedure you followed during the lab, what you learned, and how the experience ties into the material you are studying. Write down any questions you have about what you did, the results you obtained, or the interpretation of the results. Discuss the questions with your teacher when you have a chance.

Tip 87: Find out what you need to know.

If your science teachers emphasize the ability to use and understand constants and equations over memorization skills, they may provide certain information on quizzes and exams.

If you are faced with a long list of numbers and formulas, ask your teacher what you will be responsible for remembering. If your teacher is planning on supplying you with an equation sheet or other reference material, focus your study time and energy on learning to use the information.

Tip 88: Look for real life examples.

Science is a subject that applies to nearly every aspect of life. If you find it hard to stay motivated in your science class, look around you for examples that can help cement your understanding of concepts and make what you are studying more relevant to your life. For example:

- The spin cycle of a washing machine uses centrifugal force to remove water from wet clothes.

- Modern dog breeds are the result of genetics and selective breeding.

- Because of relative humidity, heated air can make hair frizzy and dehydrate skin.

- As described by the Ideal Gas Law, heating water in a teapot causes a buildup of pressure which eventually leads to the characteristic sputtering and whistling.

Researching how the science you are learning in class influences the world around you can help make the material more interesting and less abstract.

Case Study: Shaina Ewing

Shaina Ewing

High School Student

I arrange the material we talk about in class in a color-coded notebook. I make a table of contents of the notes that tells me what section each colored tab relates to. On open-note tests, all the information is organized and I can get what I need quickly.

CLASSIFIED CASE STUDIES
™
directly from the experts

CRAMMING

Starting early and working consistently are important elements of academic success. Students who consistently wait until the night before an assignment is due or a test is scheduled take risks, including the following:

Lower grades: Trying to finish an assignment or learn material quickly means there is less time to proofread, review, and prepare learning tools such as outlines, flip books, cause and effect puzzles, and slide cards.

Higher stress: Students who need to complete large amounts of work in small periods of time may feel pressured and anxious.

The domino effect: Taking time away from studying one subject to cram for a test or finish an assignment may have long-term time management consequences.

Poor health: High stress levels and altered sleep routines can lower students' immune responses.

Despite the risks, many students still find themselves in a situation where they have to cram.

What is Cramming?

Cramming means trying to finish a large number of study tasks in a short amount of time. Tip 35 covered the process involved in dividing a large project such as preparing for a test or writing a term paper, into tasks. The tasks related to studying for a science test might include:

- Reading the chapter

- Outlining the chapter

- Organizing class lecture notes

- Preparing flash cards for vocabulary words

- Reviewing diagrams

- Reviewing laboratory notes

When spread out over a week, this task list seems reasonable. If students try to cram all the tasks into a single night, they may need to devote a limited amount of time to each task or even skip some tasks.

Why Do Students Cram?

There are many excuses people give for cramming, including:

- "I just did not have enough time to study before."

- "I work better under pressure."

- "I had more important things to do."

- "I just had trouble getting started."

- "I did not realize I had that much to do."

- "I was working on something else all week."

- "It was more important for me to study for a different exam or complete another assignment."

- "The weather was just too pretty to be inside studying."

Each of these excuses boils down to one of these reasons:

Unforeseen circumstances: A personal crisis can cause upheaval in the most structured schedule. Good time managers plan extra time for emergencies, but may still find themselves in occasional situations that require cramming.

Poor time management habits: Not understanding or practicing effective scheduling and project management skills can leave students short on time.

Disinterest: A student not interested in a particular subject or school in general is not likely to make daily studying a priority.

Misconceptions: Some students do not think the cons of cramming apply to them. They may believe that they perform better under tight deadlines.

Tip 89: It is better not to cram, but recognize that you may need to on occasion.

If you are an effective time manager, you may think that you will never need to cram. Even if you are the type of student who begins studying the minute a test date is announced, do not skip this chapter. If one of the following happens, you may need to know how to fit the most studying possible in the least amount of time:

Overscheduling: If your cheerleading team pulls a surprise win in the regional competition and is preparing for states the same week you are scheduled to work late at your part-time job, you may not have enough hours available to study for an upcoming biology test.

Miscommunication: Everyone makes mistakes. You may have written down "May 15" as the deadline for a major project when it was due May 5. Perhaps a classmate told you the teacher had given an extension on an assignment, and you mistakenly assumed the new deadline was for the entire class. If you planned your study scheduled based on incomplete or erroneous information, you may find yourself scrambling to prepare for a test or finish an assignment at the last minute.

Personal emergencies: Illness, injuries, and relationship problems can make schedules seem unimportant. No matter what your personal turmoil, you still have to face tests and assignment deadlines.

This chapter is targeted especially toward students who never cram. They already know the benefits of a well-planned routine, but if their best-laid intentions fall apart they may not have the tools needed to hold a successful emergency study session.

Cramming for a test should be the last resort. Even if you need to cram on occasion, do not make it a habit.

Tip 90: Avoid using stimulants.

When trying to prepare for an exam or finish an assignment in an unreasonably short time, sleep may not seem as important as having a few extra hours of work time. Some students are tempted to use over the counter or prescription stimulants to try to stay awake and mentally sharp. These drugs are sometimes called "study drugs," "cramming drugs," or "smarties."

Using chemicals to extend your work session is a bad idea. Stimulants can have adverse effects on your health, including:

Exacerbation of existing medical conditions: If you have Tourette's syndrome, glaucoma, depression, a seizure disorder, anxiety, a liver or gastrointestinal disorder, motor tics, or a history of drug use, "study drugs" can worsen your symptoms. If you are taking a prescription drug, stimulants may interfere with their functions.

Addiction: Studies suggest that the most common stimulants are addictive. Stopping use can cause withdrawal symptoms such as depression, irritability, fatigue, and insomnia.

Anxiety: Stimulants can cause nervousness and agitation.

Headaches: After taking "cramming drugs," students may have blunt or sharp headaches that make concentration difficult.

Delusions: In addition to visual hallucinations, stimulants can produce paranoia.

Dizziness: Stimulants can make students feel lightheaded and shaky.

Blurred vision: Students who take stimulants may find it difficult to focus clearly enough to read their textbook or notes.

Increases blood pressure: Stimulant use may increase your blood pressure to the point that you are at risk for a stroke or heart attack.

Irregular heart beat: "Study drugs" can cause hearts to miss beats or change tempo rapidly.

The small chance that stimulants and supplements will increase your test grade is just not worth jeopardizing your health.

Tip 91: Do not try to memorize everything.

Students who cram have to study in survival mode. They need to prioritize, cut corners, and make decisions about how to best make use of limited time.

The first step in cramming for a test is realizing that you will not be able to learn everything well. This leaves you with two choices. You can try to cover everything briefly or you can focus your efforts on select information.

If you try to learn everything, odds are good that you will forget a large portion of what you studied before the test. It is difficult to retain information after only seeing it for a short time. What you do remember, you will not know well.

In most situations, it is better to concentrate on a few important concepts and try to learn them as completely as possible in the time available.

Start your marathon study session by surveying the material. Take a quick look at your class notes and the textbook chapters the test will cover. Make a list of the main headings of the text and the ideas your teacher devoted the most class time to explaining. Review earlier assignments and tests. Add the concepts covered in the previous work to your list.

Depending of the class you are cramming for, your list may include:

- Plot lines and character sketches of novels and short stories

- Diagrams of scientific processes or cycles

- Timelines and maps related to historic events

- Conjugations and vocabulary lists for foreign languages

- Formulas and steps for solving math problems

Once you have a list of the core ideas that are likely to be covered in the test, get to work. Spend 15 minutes on each concept before you move on to the next. After you reach the bottom of you list, start again. When studying the major concept, pay particular attention to related:

- Examples in your notes or textbook

- Diagrams

- Vocabulary words

   ➛   Homework assignments

   ➛   Lists

Repeat the process until your study time is over or you feel comfortable with this broad view of the material. If you have time after mastering the key material, you can move on to secondary information.

Tip 92: Study with a pencil in your hand.

When cramming for an exam, you are faced with the challenge of learning as much as possible, as thoroughly as you can, in a minimal amount of time. You can study more efficiently if you take notes on the material as you review it.

Take notes even if you have already outlined what you are reading. Copy important parts of your lecture note. Rework examples and assigned problems. The more you write down, the more you will remember.

Tip 93: Realize that what you learn in one night is unlikely to stay with you.

One reason that cramming is not an efficient study method is because you are unlikely to learn much in the process. The information you cover in a cramming session will not be incorporated into your long-term memory.

If you need to know the information for a standardized test, cumulative midterm or final exam, or future class, be sure to schedule time in your future study sessions to learn the material at a more relaxed pace.

Tip 94: Review what went wrong.

Cramming for a test, especially if it turns into an all-night event, is not likely to be something you want to repeat. After your test, look over your work, school, and personal schedule. Try to identify the circumstances that put you in the position of having to cram. Determine ways you can better manage your time to minimize the chances of having to cram in the future.

During your reflection, consider the following questions:

- What events led to the need to cram for the test?

- When could you have fit in more study time in the days before you decided to cram?

- Did your attitude toward the subject influence your need to cram?

- Do you have too many activities in your schedule?

- Do you need to reorganize your responsibilities to make more time to study?

- What steps can you take to try to avoid cramming in the future?

Case Study: Asia Richardson

Asia Richardson

College Resident Assistant

Do not wait too long to study for a quiz or test. At the minimum, give yourself two days to go over all your notes.

CLASSIFIED CASE STUDIES
™
directly from the experts

Exams & Standardized Tests

Tests can be the moment of truth for a student. Weeks of study and preparation lead to a single grade. Before and after a test, students may experience emotions such as:

Anxiety: Students may wonder if they studied the right material, if the exam will be difficult to understand, if they will make mistakes, or if other students will perform well.

Confidence: Students who think they prepared well for the exam may feel sure that they will earn a high score.

Disappointment: Some students may regret not studying more or different material.

Relief: Students with large emotional or time investments in the test may be glad that the preparation period is over.

The tips in this chapter can help you understand the importance of exams, minimize test-related stress, and keep the experience in perspective.

What Tests Do and Do Not Show

Tests may be designed for specific purposes, such as:

- To assess a student's understanding of a concept or set of concepts

- To determine how well a student can recall a series of facts

- To measure a student's proficiency at a skill or activity

Many factors may influence how a student performs on a test. Students' health, sleep schedules, stress levels, and comfort can affect their ability to do their best on an exam.

A test score is just a snapshot of a student's ability to answer a certain set of questions during a specific hour of a particular day. It may not reflect how well the student understands the material, how much time was invested in studying for the test, or how smart the student is.

Types of Test Questions

The word "question" is used as a broad term to refer to any exercise used in a test. Test questions do not have to end with question marks. A question may be instructions for writing an essay, a word to define, or a series of terms that should be matched with their descriptions.

A test may contain one or more of the following types of questions: essay, true or false, multiple choice, short answer, matching, or fill-in-the-blank.

Essay

Essay questions ask students to explain concepts or solve problems using the students' own words. Answers to essay questions may range from a paragraph to several pages long. Teachers may give students partial credit for incomplete answers to essay questions.

SAMPLE ESSAY QUESTIONS

What role do dreams play in *The Return of the Native*?

Explain how human actions could reduce pollution at each stage of the water cycle.

Describe the key points leading up to the Battle of Bunker Hill.

True or False

True and false sections consist of statements. Students need to determine whether or not each statement is valid.

SAMPLE TRUE OR FALSE QUESTIONS

True or false, apples and strawberries are in the same taxonomic family.

Circle T or F. The sinking of the Lusitania was the main trigger for the United State's involvement in World War I.

State if the following sentence is true or false. If it is false, rewrite it so that it is true. According to Roman mythology, Zeus was the son of Chronos.

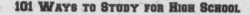

Multiple Choice

In a multiple choice question, students are asked to choose the best response from a list of possible answers.

Sample Multiple Choice Questions

In Homer's *The Odyssey*, which of the following phrases is used to describe Athena?

    a) "The goddess with the flashing eyes."
    b) "The favored daughter of Zeus."
    c) "The goddess of the gentle hands."
    d) "She who flies with the owl."

Which of following is not part of an atom?

    a) protons
    b) neutrons
    c) electrons
    d) photons

Which category of figurative language relates to repeated vowels sounds?

    a) consonance
    b) assonance
    c) onomatopoeia
    d) alliteration

Adenine is which type of molecule?

    a) nucleotide
    b) nucleoside
    c) nucleic acid
    d) oligosaccharide

Short Answer

Like essay questions, short answer questions challenge students to compose their own responses to a question. Short answer questions require a few words to a few sentences to answer.

SAMPLE SHORT ANSWER QUESTIONS

According to Piaget, a child who has just reached the object permanence milestone is in which period of development?

List confederate generals active during the American Civil War.

Briefly explain bacteria's role in the nitrogen cycle.

Matching

In matching sections, students must pick the term or statement in one column which best corresponds to the term or statement in another column.

Directions: For each term on the left, write the letter of the correct description.

1. Cataracts _____

2. Chalazion _____

3. Glaucoma _____

4. Hordeolum _____

5. Hyperopia _____

a. A cyst caused by an obstruction in the meibomian gland

b. Stye

c. Elevated intraocular pressure

d. Farsightedness

e. Cloudiness in the lens of the eye which alters visual perception

Fill-in-the-Blank

To answer fill-in-the-blank problems, students must write a word or phrase to complete a sentence or answer a question.

SAMPLE FILL-IN-THE-BLANK QUESTIONS

Directions: Complete each sentence.

1. _____ refers to the number of pixels that a screen can display at once.

2. The speed of line printers is measured in _____ per minute.

3. The two main organizational units of a computer's central processing unit (CPU) are the _____ and the _____.

4. Computers that have hundreds to thousands of CPUs are configured using an approach called _____ _____.

Nonstandard Formats

Some teachers add crossword puzzles, word finds, and acrostics to tests. These nonstandard formats are often variations of other types of questions. For example, a crossword puzzle that is a combination of short answer and fill-in-the-blank questions might be used on a test.

You may find it difficult to answer a particular test question even if you understand the information addressed. Each type of question has its own potential pitfalls. Understanding the hazard zones for each class of questions can help you avoid them.

Some of the reasons students may lose points when answering essay questions include:

Not understanding the question: To correctly answer an essay question, you need to understand exactly what is being asked. For how to translate essay question vocabulary, review Tip 74.

Answering a different question: Avoid performing logical gymnastics to twist the question into a topic you are more prepared to write about. For example, if the question asks about the imagery in Silas Marner, make sure everything you write in your answer relates to that subject. Do not veer into other books or themes unless they directly relate to the question.

Babbling: If you feel rushed to finish an essay question, your answer may read more like a jumbled list of examples and explanations than a coherent composition. To help make your answer more organized, take a few minutes before writing to jot down a short outline of your answer.

Poor grammar: Some teachers deduct points for misspelled words or grammatical errors. Proofread your test before you turn it in.

Answering only part of the question: Essay questions may have multiple parts. After you write an answer, reread the question to make sure you covered everything that was asked.

True or false questions also have some specific hazards. When answering true or false questions, be sure to:

Read every word of the question: Modifiers like "not," "all," "none," "few," "usually," "always," and "never" can change the answer of a true or false statement.

Be prepared to support your case: Do not write "true" or "false" because of a gut feeling. Think about examples that support your answer.

When faced with multiple-choice questions, remember the following:

Read all the possible answers: Do not simply select the first answer that appears to be correct. There may be a better answer later in the list.

Know the rules before you guess: Some teachers and standardized test publishers take points off for wrong answers on multiple-choice questions to discourage random guessing. For example, if each correct multiple-choice question is worth five points, an incorrect answer may reduce the test score by one point. Make sure you understand the grading policy before you guess on a multiple-choice question. Even if you are penalized for incorrect answers, it may be worth the risk if you can narrow your options by recognizing one or more of the wrong choices.

Fill-in-the-blank and short-answer questions are straight forward, but there are some tricks that might help you avoid giving wrong answers, including the following.

Look at tenses: The verb form of the question can indicate whether the teacher is looking for one or several answers. The use of "an" rather than "a" in front of a blank indicates that the answer begins with a vowel.

The size of the blank: While not a hard and fast rule, the amount of room the teacher provided after a question can indicate how long an appropriate answer should be.

When completing matching exercises, it is important to realize that the corresponding answer to a question may not be the exact definition. There may also be two or more answers that could fit for a particular question. In these cases, you need to find the best answer among the choices. To help with this, read over both columns before you start writing answers. Fill in the answers you are certain of and then reason through the remaining questions. Unless you are told otherwise in the directions, do not assume that each answer can only be used once. As with fill-in-the-blank and short answer questions, sometimes tenses can provide hints for selecting correct answers.

STANDARDIZED TESTS

A standardized test is simply a test that is given to a broad group of people. You may need to take a standardized test to gain admittance to a college, graduate from high school, or get a job. Some school systems give standardized tests to students periodically through their academic career to gauge how well the school faculty and policies support the students' mastery of basic skills. Standardized tests that high school students may take include:

The Armed Services Vocational Aptitude Battery (ASVAB): The ASVAB is used to determine if applicants are eligible to enlist in the armed forces and to qualify applicants for military occupational specialties.

The SAT Reasoning Test and the ACT: The ACT and the SAT attempt to assess students' critical thinking skills. Many colleges consider ACT and SAT scores when granting admission and awarding scholarships.

The Preliminary SAT/National Merit Qualifying Test (PSAT/NMSQT): An SAT practice test and the qualifying exam for the National Merit Scholarship Corporation scholarship program.

Advanced Placement (AP) Tests: Each AP test focuses on a single subject, such as calculus, biology, or music theory. Colleges may grant credit based on a student's grade on an AP test.

College Level Examination Program (CLEP): CLEP allows students to earn credit or advanced standing at post-secondary schools by passing subject-specific tests.

State graduation examinations: Some school districts require students to pass a standardized test to earn a high school diploma.

Standardized exams present different challenges than tests students take in high school classes. Because much can be riding on a single standardized test, students may feel stressed to perform their best. Some material on the test may not be familiar to them, and they will not have the opportunity to defend the thought processes that led them to choose one answer over another.

PREPARATION LEADS TO CONFIDENCE

Test preparation includes more than just learning the material that will be covered on the test. You should also become familiar with the likely format of the test. Being well prepared for a test also means taking care of yourself and learning how to relax.

Whether preparing for a weekly test in art history or a standardized test to earn college credit, the hints in this chapter can give you more confidence and less anxiety for your next exam.

Tip 95: Consider previous tests.

When studying for an exam, look over the class's past quizzes and tests. Does your teacher rely mainly on multiple choice, essay, short answer, fill-in-the-blank, true or false, or nonstandard format questions? Are the questions more focused on the broad topics or on the smaller details? Does the teacher write the test or use one connected to the class textbook?

When preparing for a standardized test, take at least one practice test to help you become familiar with the format. You can purchase study tools for many standardized tests. Free sample tests may also be available from the testing organization. Some online resources for free standardized test preparations tools are listed in the table below.

Free Practice for Standardized Tests	
PSAT/NMSQT	http://www.collegeboard.com/student/testing/psat/prep.html
SAT	http://www.collegeboard.com/student/testing/sat/prep_one/critical_reading.html
AP	http://www.collegeboard.com/student/testing/ap/prep.html
CLEP	http://www.collegeboard.com/student/testing/clep/exams.html
ACT	http://www.actstudent.org/sampletest/index.html
ASVAB	http://www.military.com/ASVAB

Tip 96: Create your own study guides.

Use your textbook, lecture notes, and the previous tips in this book to write your own study guide. A good study guide can be an effective tool even before you finish creating it. The process of reviewing information, determining what is likely to be on the test, organizing it in a logical format, and writing the study guide can go a long way toward helping you master the material.

A good study guide should be:

Legible: Avoid wasting valuable study time trying to decipher your writing.

Accurate: Avoid studying incorrect information. Double check the material you include in your study guide.

Portable: Reviewing your study guide in several short spurts throughout the days leading up to your exam can be more effective than sitting down for a marathon study session. A conveniently sized study guide will allow you to study on the bus, during work breaks, or between classes.

Organized: Try to find logical groupings for the data you include in your study guide. Organization will make the information easier to study, and it will help you understand the relationships between the concepts you are learning.

Concise: Do not load your study guide with details that are unlikely to be on the test.

There is no perfect template for an effective study guide. The best format is the one that works for you. The following tips explain techniques that you can incorporate into your study guide:

- Tip 18: Auditory learners: Recite and repeat.

- Tip 19: Visual learners: Sketch out concepts.

- Tip 20: Tactile learners: Let your fingers help you learn.

- Tip 31: Create outlines to help you read for content.

- Tip 54: Do not study from the book.

- Tip 78: Create and use flashcards.

- Tip 84: Study diagrams.

- Tip 85: Create mnemonics to make memorization tasks easier.

Tip 97: Take practice tests.

Practicing your test-taking skills can help you feel less anxious in high-pressure exam situations and reveal strengths and weaknesses in your understanding of the material. You may be able to obtain practice tests from several sources, including:

Your book: Your textbook may include practice tests.

Your teacher: Ask your teacher if a sample test is available in the teacher edition of the textbook.

A friend: Prepare a test based on the material and ask a classmate to do the same, and then exchange tests.

Yourself: Use your study guide, textbook, and notes to create your own test. Do not worry about making an answer key; just write questions based on the material that will be covered on the upcoming test. Wait a day or two before taking your self-written test so you are using your long-term memory for your responses. After taking the practice test, check it against your notes.

Homework and quizzes: Get questions from your homework and quizzes and rearrange to create a practice test. Use graded papers as answer keys.

The Internet: If you are studying for a standardized test, you may be able to find practice tests on the Internet. Some textbook publishers provide supplemental materials such as sample exams on their Web sites.

To get the most out of a practice test, try to duplicate the conditions under which you will be taking the exam. Give yourself the same amount of time you will have in class. Try to find a quiet place where you can concentrate. Do not use any tools that will not be available to you during the test. For example, if the exam is going to be closed-notes, and closed-book, resist the urge to look up a hint to a confusing problem.

Wait until you have completed the test before correcting your work. Use your performance on the practice test to guide your studying. If you missed a question or got the correct answer because of a lucky guess, review that concept thoroughly.

Tip 98: Prepare for standardized tests all year long.

The SAT, ACT, ASVAB, and PSAT/NMSQT tests are designed to test what students have learned throughout their academic careers. The AP and CLEP tests attempt to gauge how well students have mastered material during one or two semesters. Because of the wide range of information standardized tests cover, students should not expect to study for them in only two or three weeks. To perform their best on standardized tests, students should prepare throughout the year.

This does not mean you need to spend an hour everyday learning vocabulary words or performing math drills. The following suggestions can work together to help you prepare for standardized tests:

Maintain a regular study routine: By completing your school assignments, you are learning material that may show up on standardized tests.

Read: Reading for pleasure can help develop vocabulary, critical thinking, and logic.

Pay attention in class: Even if your teacher is not going to test you on information covered in class, it might show up on a standardized test.

Ask questions: Strive to understand the concepts presented in class, not just memorize the information that will be on exams.

Tip 99: Brain dump.

You may encounter information that you just need to sit down and memorize for an exam. Whether it is a scientific constant, a mathematical equation, a historical date, or a foreign language verb conjugation, data that you learn by rote can cause stress during tests. You may worry that you will forget the information before you have a chance to use it, or that your recall will be faulty. This anxiety can distract you and prevent you from performing your best on the rest of the exam.

One way to prevent the added stress of trying to keep important information in your head while taking a test is to "brain dump," which means to write the data down so that you do not have to worry about remembering it.

To avoid even the appearance of cheating, wait to brain dump until after test papers have been handed out and you are allowed to start working. If you have been given scratch paper or are

...lowed to use your own paper to work out answers to test questions, write the information on that. Otherwise, ask your teacher or test proctor if you can brain dump on the back or in the margin of the test paper.

Tip 100: Relax.

Class and standardized tests are important events that should not be taken lightly, but worrying too much about a single exam can inhibit your performance and cause physical strain.

Because tension can lead to headaches, backaches, reduced energy, lowered ability to concentrate, and diminished problem solving abilities, it can interfere with your ability to do your best on a test. Investing a few minutes in focused relaxation before you take an important or stressful test can have many benefits, including:

- Lowered blood pressure and heart rate

- Increased blood flow

- Diminished muscle tension

- Improved ability to handle intense situations

- Elevated energy levels

There are a variety of relaxation exercises that may help you calm down before a test. You can find out about specific techniques by taking classes, talking with a doctor or counselor, reading books, or experimenting to find out what works best for you. Most relaxation techniques can be classified as visualization, progressive muscle relaxation, or autogenic relaxation.

Visualization: Visualization techniques involve picturing relaxing environments and tranquil situations. Tastes, aromas, textures, and sounds can be used to enhance the calming effect. For example, a student may use visualization to help relax before a test by imagining the gentle lap of ocean waves over a quiet beach. Rubbing a seashell, lighting a scented candle, or listening to wind chimes can add to the experience.

Progressive Muscle Relaxation: Progressive muscle relaxation techniques focus on increasing muscle awareness. This is achieved by contracting and then relaxing each muscle group. An example of a progressive muscle relaxation technique is to clench muscles for six seconds, then letting them relax for 40 seconds. A student might begin by focusing on their hand muscles, then move on to the arms, chest, and neck. Finally, the student could repeat the contracting and relaxing pattern with the face muscles.

Autogenic Relaxation: Autogenic relaxation combines visualization and progressive muscle practices. These techniques may involve thinking about serene images, repeating phrases, controlling breathing, and forcing muscles to relax.

Exams can be stressful enough without the added tension that can come from worrying about factors you have no control over. Releasing the following fears can help you be more relaxed when you face your next test:

Will other people score better than you? You have no power over how your classmates study for an exam, what they have for breakfast on test day, or how well they slept the night before. Instead of wasting energy by worrying about how your score will compare to other people's scores, concentrate on doing your best work.

Will the test cover material you did not study? What you identify as the significant topics of a unit may differ from what your teacher considers important. Learn as much of the material as possible, but recognize your time and energy limits.

Will you make simple mistakes? Paying close attention to each question and checking your work can help minimize errors, but accidents can still happen. Commit to doing your best to prevent mistakes, but do not berate yourself if you make an arithmetic error, circle the wrong letter on a multiple choice question, or accidentally skip a problem.

How hard will the teacher grade? Grading standards can vary widely between instructors. An answer to an essay question that earns full credit from one teacher may be considered only partially correct by another. Instead of worrying about how your teacher will grade your exam, concentrate on making each answer as complete and well-crafted as possible.

There are many things you can do to prepare for an exam. Do not squander study time worrying about issues that are out of your control.

Tip 101: Use a good test score as momentum.

Preparing for an exam can be stressful, time consuming, and physically tiring. The payoff for the investment is a better shot at earning a good score on the test.

A successful exam performance is a reason to celebrate, but do not let it become an excuse to become complacent. See your grade as proof that steady work produces results. View each academic victory as another step to helping you reach long-term goals.

CONCLUSION

Succeeding in school is like running a marathon, learning to play a musical instrument, or growing a beautiful garden -- it takes more than desire to achieve. With steady work, thoughtful use of appropriate techniques, and good time management practices, you can improve your study habits and live up to your academic potential. The tips in this book are not shortcuts for getting good grades, but they can help you learn more effectively and complete your assignments efficiently.

Learning is not a linear journey. There may be times when you have to take a few steps back to keep progressing. You are likely to encounter some bumps as you work toward graduation. Life changes such as a new sibling, moving, or serious illness can make it hard to find the time and motivation to study.

Do not let a temporary situation become a permanent excuse for not reaching your goals.

High school is a chance that never comes again. The decisions you make now can influence the college you go to and the financial aid you will receive. The time-management skills you develop can be applied to your future studies or career. The information you learn through your studies may benefit you throughout your life in ways you never expected.

Following a steady study routine is a decision. It can be difficult to choose to invest in your future when you would rather watch television, play on the Internet, or visit with friends. When you hit a bump or feel a dip in your motivation level, remind yourself why you want to earn good grades. Reread Chapters 1 and 2. Think about the long-term results of your actions.

Parents, teachers, and school administrators all have important roles to play in helping you learn, but the ultimate responsibility for your education rests on your shoulders.

BIBLIOGRAPHY

Biographies of Women Mathematicians. Larry Riddle. 2007. Agnes Scott College. 30 Mar. 2008 < **http://www.agnesscott.edu/Lriddle/women/women.htm**>.

Bly, Robert. *The Copywriter's Handbook.* New York: Henry Holt and Company, 2005.

Fry, Ron. *How to Study.* 6th ed. Clifton Park: Thomson Delmar Learning, 2005.

Herbert Earle Buchanan. Edward A. Allen. 2007. *Encyclopedia of Arkansas History & Culture Project.* 30 Mar. 2008 < **http://www.encyclopediaofarkansas.net/encyclopedia/entry-detail.aspx?entryID=415**>

Hodges, John C., et al. *Harbrace College Handbook.* 12th ed. Fort Worth: Harcourt, 1994.

Jones, Betty. *Comprehensive Medical Terminology.* 2nd ed. Clifton Park: Thomas Delmar Learning, 2003.

Kornhauser, Arthur. *How to Study*. 3rd ed. Chicago: University of Chicago Press, 1993.

Luckie, William R., and Wood Smethurst. *Study Power: Study Skills to Improve Your Learning and Your Grades*. Manchester: Brookline, 1998.

Mama Lisa's World: Nursery Rhymes and Songs of All Nations. 2008. Lisa Yannucci. 29 Mar. 2008 **<http://www.mamalisa.com>**.

Mathematicians of the African Diaspora. Scott W. Williams. 2002. University at Buffalo, The State University of New York. 30 Mar. 2008 **< http://www.math.buffalo.edu/mad/madgreatest.html>**.

Menz, Deb. *Color Works*. Loveloand: Interweave Press, 2004.

National Geographic Society. *National Geographic Atlas for Young Explorers*. Washington, D.C.: National Geographic Society, 1999.

The New Workplace Mix. Stephanie Armour. 2005. USA Today. 3 Apr. 2008 **<http://www.usatoday.com/money/workplace/2005-11-06-gen-y_x.htm>**.

Nickerson, Robert. *Business and Information Systems*. 2nd ed. Upper Saddle River, NJ: Prentice Hall, 2001.

Relaxation Techniques: *Learn Ways to Calm Your Stress*. Mayo Clinic Staff. 2007. Mayo Foundation for Medical Education and Research. 2 Apr. 2008 **<http://www.mayoclinic.com/health/re-laxation-technique/SR00007#>**.

Robinson, Adam. *What Smart Students Know*. New York: Three Rivers Press, 1993.

Rozakis, Laurie. *Super Study Skills*. New York: Scholastic Reference, 2002.

--*Test Taking Strategies and Study Skills for the Utterly Confused*. New York: McGraw-Hill, 2003.

Sussman, Steve, Mary Ann Pentz, Donna Spruijt-Metz, and Toby Miller. *"Misuse of 'Study Drugs:' Prevalence, Consequences, and Implications for Policy."* Substance Abuse Treatment, Prevention, and Policy. 2006, 1:15.

Swick, Edward. *The Everything Learning German Book: Speak, Write, and Understand Basic German in No Time*. Avon: Adams Media, 2003.

Writing Essay Exams. 2004. Purdue University Online Writing Lab. 31 Mar. 2008 < **http://owl.english.purdue.edu/handouts/general/gl_essay.html**>.

Author Dedication & Biography

I would like to thank all of the teachers and students who took time from their busy lives to be interviewed for this book, Angela Adams at Atlantic Publishing for her help with this project, my sons Alex and Daniel for understanding when I had to work, and my husband David for his unending confidence in me.

Janet Engle writes books and articles about science, business, and personal growth. She lives with her husband, two sons, two cats, and one extraordinarily hyperactive beagle. When she is not writing, she enjoys running, woodcarving, knitting, and playing the flute.

INDEX